M02 40004 56814

2001

D0844801

SAINTS AND FIREWORKS
RELIGION AND POLITICS IN RURAL MALTA

LONDON SCHOOL OF ECONOMICS
MONOGRAPHS ON SOCIAL ANTHROPOLOGY

Managing Editor: Anthony Forge

The Monographs on Social Anthropology were established in 1940 and aim to publish results of modern anthropological research of primary interest to specialists.

The continuation of the series was made possible by a grant in aid from the Wenner-Gren Foundation for Anthropological Research. and more recently by a further grant from the Governors of the London School of Economics and Political Science.

The Monographs are under the direction of an Editorial Board associated with the Department of Anthropology of the London School of Economics and Political Science.

St George and partisans

LONDON SCHOOL OF ECONOMICS
MONOGRAPHS ON SOCIAL ANTHROPOLOGY
No. 30

SAINTS
AND FIREWORKS

Religion and Politics in Rural Malta

BY

JEREMY BOISSEVAIN

HN
660.5
M32
B6

20013

UNIVERSITY OF LONDON
THE ATHLONE PRESS
NEW YORK: HUMANITIES PRESS INC.

Published by
THE ATHLONE PRESS
UNIVERSITY OF LONDON
at 2 Gower Street, London, WCI

Distributed by Tiptree Book Services Ltd
Tiptree, Essex

Australia and New Zealand
Melbourne University Press

Canada
Oxford University Press
Toronto

First edition, 1965
First paperback edition, with corrections and a postscript, 1969

© *Jeremy Boissevain,* 1965, 1969

485 19630 1

First Printed in Great Britain by
WESTERN PRINTING SERVICES LTD
BRISTOL

Reprinted by photolitho by
WILLIAM CLOWES AND SONS LTD
LONDON AND BECCLES

TO INGA

Mingħajr qaddisin ma titlax il-ġenna
'You can't get to heaven without saints.'
Maltese proverb

Preface

This study was carried out and written shortly before Malta became an independent nation. Its purpose is to present a descriptive analysis of Maltese village politics. In many respects these are quite unusual, for in Malta, which has been administered as a fortress for the last four centuries, there are no village headmen, mayors or councillors to serve as links between their villages and the central government. But in spite of the highly centralized administration certain activities in the villages do play a part in the decision of both local and national issues, though at first sight they may not seem to be closely connected with politics as this is usually conceived. These are political activities, for as Prof. Lucy Mair has observed, politics is concerned with the ways persons and groups compete to influence the outcome of disputes and community decisions in accordance with their own interests.[1] The central problem can thus be divided into three major parts: first, to explore the relations between competing persons and groups; second, to examine the nature of the issues which concern them and the community; and third, to trace the channels through which they bring influence to bear on those who make the decisions.

After a brief sketch of Malta in time and space, I examine successively the articulation of the State, the Church and the political parties with the villages, the ties of neighbourhood and family, the social composition of the villages, and the basis of leadership. Against this background I show how issues which originate within the Church, and in particular over the cult of saints, affect village social organization. I then look at the effects of disputes arising out of issues of national policy. Finally, I examine the channels of influence open to the villagers.

Throughout this study I have been exclusively concerned with describing and analysing the political life of the villages of Malta and Gozo. But it has occasionally been necessary for me to make brief excursions into the field of national politics, for because of Malta's smallness, national political disputes swiftly become issues

[1] Lucy Mair, *Primitive Government* (London, Penguin Books, 1962), p. 10.

which divide the villages. I have therefore presented the current political and religious issues in Malta as concisely as possible, and have made no attempt to evaluate or to pass judgement on the policies of State, Church or political party. Consequently, any attempt to put the facts contained herein to polemical use is likely to distort them.

Though I lived in Malta during 1957 and 1958, this study is based on the research I carried out there from July 1960 to September 1961 under a grant from the Colonial Social Science Research Council, to whom I am most grateful. The terms of reference on which the research was based, and the form this final report has assumed, were dictated solely by my personal interests; my work was neither carried out on behalf of, nor a report to, a government.

My wife and daughters were with me during the entire period of fieldwork, and their encouragement and interest as well as the many friends they made were a great asset. We spent our first five months in Farruġ and the last eight months in Kortin. These are not the real names of the villages, for the inhabitants of neither seek recognition. Indeed, throughout this study I have been at pains to avoid any indiscretion which would repay most shamefully our special debt of gratitude to friends and neighbours for their hospitality and good humour in the face of our ignorance of their customs. For the same reason, the names of many of the persons and saints who figure in this account have been altered.

I chose to work in Farruġ because it is one of the villages divided by competing band clubs, and among other things I was particularly interested in the part this unusual rivalry plays in village politics. With a population of approximately 1,400, it is one of the smaller Maltese villages. We later moved to Kortin, a village of almost 5,000, since its size and the fact that it is not divided by band club rivalry provided an interesting contrast to Farruġ. Available housing determined the choice of these particular two villages from among the many that would have met my requirements. Besides detailed research in these villages, I carried out comparative studies into the general organization, leadership and patterns of conflict of 12 other communities. In this work Mr. Edward Micallef was my very able research assistant for three months. I chose 11 of these villages by stratifying all villages in Malta and Gozo according to population and then drawing out a

30 per cent random sample. Those selected this way were Balzan, Dingli, Gudja, Għarb, Għargħur, Mosta, Qala, Qrendi, Xagħra, Żebbuġ (Malta) and Żurrieq. I also chose Sliema, a large suburb, to provide a special contrast to the villages. Thus the general statements I make about Maltese villages are based on a fairly wide cross-section.

Thanks to the patient teaching of our friends Francis and Evelyn Chetcuti during the year preceding fieldwork, I was able to begin to work in Maltese soon after my arrival. Much of my work, however, was done in English, which many informants spoke fluently.

I also wish to express my thanks to Mr. Trafford Smith, former Lieutenant-Governor of Malta; to Mr. Maurice Abela, the Principal Government Statistician, and Chev. Paul Naudi, Director of Information, and their assistants; to Dr. V. De Pasquale, Chev. J. Galea, Mr. E. R. Leopardi and Mr. John Bezzina of the Royal Malta Library; to the Revs. Joseph Ghigo S.J., Paul Pace, Paul Said, Joseph Theuma, Benjamin Tonna, Charles Vella and Anton Xiberras, and to the Hon. A. Barbara, Dr. Brian Beeley, Mr. J. Cassar Pullicino, Mr. Francis Mizzi and Mr. Joseph Muscat for their interest and help in many ways. Prof. J. Aquilina kindly allowed me to read the manuscript of his unpublished work on Maltese proverbs.

I am greatly indebted to the staff and my fellow students at the Department of Anthropology of the London School of Economics for their stimulating discussion, both formal and informal, of this material.

Finally, I wish to record here my very special thanks and obligation to Professor Lucy Mair, my academic supervisor, for the valuable criticism and patient help she gave me before and during my research and especially in analysing and writing up the material collected in the field.

Except for minor alterations, the present work is identical with the Ph.D. thesis I submitted to the University of London in November 1962.

J.B.

Départment d'Anthropologie
Université de Montréal

An Introductory Note on Maltese

Maltese is a distinct language which is morphologically related to North African Arabic but draws much of its vocabulary, syntax and idiom from Sicilian.[1] This difficult language is spoken by all classes, but it did not become an official language of the law courts until 1934, when it replaced Italian. As it has only been a written language for little more than 100 years, it does not yet have a rich literature.

In order to help the reader with the Maltese names and words that appear in the text, the following is given as a short guide to their approximate pronunciation.[2] In general, vowels have much the same sound as they do in Italian. The following consonants are pronounced as indicated: *ċ*: *ch*air; *ġ*: *g*entle; *g*: *g*ift; *h*: silent; *ħ*: aspirate; *gh*: the *għajn*, is usually silent; *j*: *y*ear; *q*: glottal stop; *x*: *sh*ine; *ż*: *z*ebra; and *z*: boo*ts*.

[1] Joseph Aquilina, *Papers in Maltese Linguistics* (Valletta, Royal University of Malta, 1961), p. 180.
[2] For the pronunciation of Maltese consult: Joseph Aquilina, *The Structure of Maltese* (Valletta, Royal University of Malta, 1959), pp. 1–17.

Contents

TABLES

PLATES

MAP

CHAPTER I
The Background

Malta and her sister islands, Gozo and Comino, lie midway between Gibraltar and Lebanon, at almost the exact geographical centre of the Mediterranean. Sicily lies just 58 miles to the north, Tripoli 220 miles due south and Tunis slightly over 200 miles to the west. The Maltese archipelago thus forms a port of call between Europe and North Africa, between the Christian and the Moslem worlds. The Maltese have been in contact with both for centuries, and the cultures of both have contributed many traits which the islanders have adapted to their own use.

Malta, the largest and southernmost island, is seventeen miles long and nine miles wide, and covers an area of 95 square miles. Gozo is only nine miles by five miles, with an area of 26 square miles. Finally, the little island of Comino, which lies in the three-mile-wide channel separating the two larger islands, has an area of one square mile.

The islands are composed entirely of tertiary limestone, and the soil consists of clays and marls. Although the land rises to a maximum of little more than 800 feet near Dingli, the terrain is varied, and often broken, with jagged escarpments falling into narrow valleys, which run out to level fields. A visitor to the islands, especially during the long dry summer, is struck at once by the absence of vegetation and the rocky aspect of the countryside. This is, in part, a false impression, for although there are few trees, rubble retaining and boundary walls hide the network of small cultivated fields. Occasionally, the dark green foliage of a carob or olive tree reaches over these stone enclosures to add a sudden splash of colour to the shimmering white-yellow of the summer landscape.

The soft yellow limestone gives a continuity to the scenery. Houses, villages and whole towns seem to grow up out of the rocky matrix from which they are built, and from which they are distinguished only by the regular outline of the buildings against

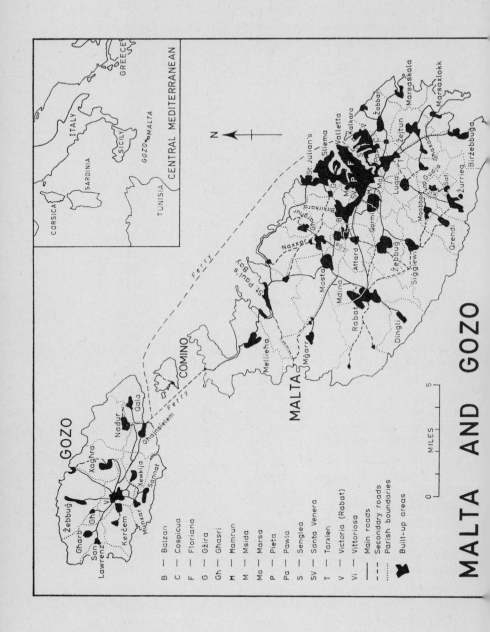

MALTA AND GOZO

the glaring skies. This stone, so characteristic of Malta, provides a gradual transition from the open country to the compact, densely populated communities in which the people live.

II

In 1960, just under 329,000 people lived on the islands' 122 square miles. This makes the Maltese archipelago, with a population density of 2,700 per square mile, one of the most thickly populated countries in the world. Slightly over half the population live in the urban area which centres on Valletta and the Grand Harbour. The rest, and the part with which this study is concerned, live in clearly separated villages and towns outside the conurbation. The population of Gozo is 28,000, and that of Comino 30.

The pressure of a numerous and fertile population on a very limited area has long been one of Malta's most serious problems. The Maltese marry rather early and, in the past, have been encouraged by the clergy and public opinion to have large families. But the Church in Malta has finally and officially recognized the problem, and recently opened a medical advisory service for married couples. During the period 1957–60, births averaged 8,600 per annum and deaths 2,820, thus the natural annual increase was about 5,780. As the net emigration during this period was 2,170 annually, the total population increased at an annual rate of approximately 3,610. Emigration, however, has taken off many of the young men and left a surplus of females. In 1960 there were 747 men between the ages of 20 and 34 for every 1,000 women in the same age group.[1]

III

Malta's documented history stretches back over a thousand years. The summary of it given here makes no pretence of originality. With but few exceptions, it is based upon the well-known published sources listed in the Bibliography. My sole object is to enable the reader to see the present political system in its historical perspective.

Throughout history, Malta has been subject to many different

[1] *Statistical Abstract of the Maltese Islands*, 1960 (Valletta, Central Office of Statistics, 1961), C, pp. 2–5.

rulers who sought to control her strategic position and fine natural harbours. Phoenicians, Carthaginians, Greeks and Romans successively occupied the islands. Although it is generally held that Malta and Gozo formed part of the Byzantine Empire, virtually nothing is known of this period of Maltese history. In A.D. 870 the Arabs occupied the islands. Two hundred years later they were replaced by the Normans under Count Roger. After the death of the last Norman king, Malta shared the fate of Sicily and passed successively to the Swabians (1194–1266), the Angevins (1266–1283), the Aragonese (1283–1410), and the Castilians. In 1530, Emperor Charles V handed over Malta and Gozo with their protesting inhabitants as a fief in perpetuity to the Sovereign Military Order of St. John of Jerusalem, a powerful body of celibate nobles vowed to helping the poor, caring for the sick and waging war on Islam. Napoleon drove out the Knights in 1798, and in 1800 Britain replaced the French. The islands were formally ceded to Britain under the terms of the Treaty of Paris in 1814. Since then they have remained a British possession.

The most important recorded event in Malta's early history was the shipwreck of St. Paul in A.D. 60.[1] During the three months he stayed in Malta, he is popularly believed to have converted the people to Christianity. Whether he converted many is a moot point, but it is a fact that he baptized the Roman governor, Publius, who became Malta's first Bishop. The Maltese are intensely proud of the apostolic origin of their religion. *Missierna San Pawl*, 'Our Father St. Paul', as he is usually called, is the principal patron saint of the islands, and the feast of his shipwreck is a national celebration. Not surprisingly, there are many local legends about him. One holds that the first people to heed his gospel were the villagers of Naxxar, and that his preaching there was heard by the people of Xewkija in Gozo.

The line of bishops established with Publius was broken during the long period of Moslem rule. Count Roger, however, re-established and endowed an episcopal see. He also helped to arrange other details of ecclesiastical organization which had lapsed while Malta was under Arab domination. The present line of Maltese bishops dates from this period.

Malta had a considerable measure of local autonomy during the Aragonese and Castilian periods. Public affairs were administered

[1] Acts 27 and 28.

by the officials of the governing body, or *Università*. This body, which met in Mdina, the old capital of the island, was composed of representatives of the nobles, learned men, secular priests, merchants and artisans elected by all the family heads in the towns and villages of Malta and Gozo. The Knights of St. John, however, severely limited the authority of the Università, and during their final years it was little more than a public corporation responsible for the importation of scarce foodstuffs.

The Order made itself responsible for local government. It controlled and financed the local militia, police, courts, water supply, public works, hospitals and charities. The government of the Order was highly centralized, and all key posts were held by Knights, though many of the lesser administrative offices were given to Maltese nobles, lawyers and clerks. The authority of the Order was made effective in the rural areas through the police and the ten Captains who were in charge of military garrisons and arsenals, located at strategic points for internal security and defence against war parties and corsairs, and were also responsible for mobilizing the militia. This paternalistic system of administration came to an abrupt end when Napoleon drove the Knights from the islands. Their departure marked the end of an era.

Napoleon remained in Malta only eight days, but they were busy days. According to Laferla, 'it is certain that no one in the space of a few days attempted more, did more and upset the Maltese more than he did.'[1] He set up a nominated council of Maltese to see to civil administration, remodelled the tribunals along French lines and established twelve municipal councils. He abolished the nobility. He closed the University, established a central technical college and founded fifteen government elementary schools. He also sent sixty sons of wealthy families off to study at republican colleges in Paris at their parents' expense.

'All this and probably much more would the Maltese have patiently tolerated,' says Laferla, 'had Napoleon not interfered with religion.'[2] For he set out to curtail the influence of the Church. He limited the jurisdiction of the Bishop to purely ecclesiastical affairs, ordered the expulsion from the islands of all non-Maltese clergy and reduced the number of clerics. He also instituted civil marriage, gave protection to the Jews and forbade

---

[1] A. V. Laferla, *The Story of Man in Malta* (3rd ed.; Malta, A. C. Aquilina and Co., 1958), p. 144.　　　　　　　　　　　　　　　　　　　　　　[2] *Ibid.*, p. 148.

the clergy to charge for their services. Finally, he decreed that no foreign power, even the Pope, might interfere in local religious administration.

By these acts, the French attacked values that were at the very foundation of the Maltese social structure. Moreover, the new government aggravated the discontent by its failure to meet its financial commitments. Less than two months later, the suppressed hostility flared into savage revolt when the authorities tried to auction off the property of the Carmelite church in Mdina. The citizens rose, massacred the town's garrison and burned their bodies. Then, led by Notary Vitale and Canon Caruana, a powerful cotton merchant who later became Bishop, they penned up the main French force under General Vaubois behind the fortifications of Valletta and the Three Cities. Two years later the French surrendered to the British force which had come to assist the Maltese.

Under British rule, Malta changed from a theocracy ruled by a religious order, to a self-governing colony with an active internal political life. Administrative posts gradually passed to Maltese hands, and today the civil service, apart from a few foreign experts, is completely Maltese. But in spite of a long flirtation with various forms of local and regional government, there are still no village mayors or councillors. The new civic committee in Gozo is an exception which will be discussed in the following chapter. Early in their rule, the British abolished the Università. To appease the wounded dignity of the nobles, they divided Malta into six districts under the nominal authority of Lords Lieutenant, chosen from the nobility. These officers were in charge of civil affairs, and presided over district courts. Each was assisted by syndics, deputies with magisterial powers, who lived in the villages. In 1839, this system of local government was abandoned as inefficient and costly, and district magistrates, also called syndics, were appointed from the class of advocates. Later, the government established district consultative committees to advise it on local needs and to coordinate health measures during epidemics. These committees were only partly successful, and were also abandoned. In 1896 the government finally abolished the office of syndic, and, in the interest of economy, closed the last district courts in 1913. After that, except for the Magistrate's Court in Gozo, the administration of justice remained centralized in Valletta.

In the early years of its rule, Britain moved slowly but firmly to restrict the authority of the Church. As one of its first steps, it imposed a mortmain law which forced the Church to sell off bequests of immovable property within one year. In 1828, it abolished the right of sanctuary and restricted the jurisdiction of the ecclesiastical courts to purely spiritual matters. Shortly afterwards, the Diocese of Malta, until then subject to the Metropolitan of Palermo, was made directly dependent on the Holy See.

In spite of the inroads Britain made on the power of the Church, the relations between the two have, on the whole, remained extremely cordial. This friendliness has been due very largely to the considerable protection which Britain has given to the Church in Malta. To begin with, it is protected from the competition of other religions. The missionary activities of groups such as the Bible Society and the Salvation Army have been severely restricted. Moreover, the government reserves the right to ban public religious ceremonies by non-Catholics if they threaten to disturb the peace. Catholic precepts regarding education and marriage are also safeguarded, for education is on Catholic religious principles, and divorce and civil marriage are not possible under Maltese law. Furthermore, the Archbishop is accorded high honour, and in the jealously guarded order of precedence he is second only to the Governor. Both the Archbishop and the Bishop of Gozo are exempt from the jurisdiction of the criminal courts.

In addition, the first Maltese elected government passed a law in 1922, declaring the Roman Catholic religion the religion of the country. Article 161 of the Malta Criminal Code makes it a criminal offence to vilify in public the Catholic religion or its ministers.[1]

Constitutional development in Malta has been a painful and slow process; for it is not a simple matter to give representative government to a fortress. The first constitution in 1835 provided for a council of government composed of five office holders, including the Governor and the Bishop, and three nominated dignitaries. Since then, there have been no less than nine different constitutions. Those promulgated before the First World War established an oligarchical system. Property restrictions on those allowed to vote and hold office resulted in elections by and for members of the landed, professional and merchant classes. Further-

[1] Act XVIII, 1933.

more, because Imperial strategic interests limited the terms of reference of these councils, the constitutions permitted only the most rudimentary form of government. Only under the 1887 Constitution did elected members outnumber official members. But this elected majority had no effective power and finally proved so awkward that in 1903 a new constitution reinstated an official majority.

After the First World War, there was popular agitation for a more liberal form of government. In 1919, the social unrest culminated in an anti-British riot during which British troops killed four demonstrators. Later that year, Britain announced that Malta would receive a more liberal constitution. The new constitution, which eventually came into force in 1921, attempted to reconcile two conflicting principles: continued British control over her strategic island-fortress, and Maltese self-government. The complicated solution which Britain adopted was dyarchy, under which effective legislative and executive power was divided between the Governor and the representatives of the Maltese people. This created two separate governments.

The Imperial Government dealt with 'Reserved Matters', which included defence, foreign relations, immigration and coinage. The Malta Government consisted of a seventeen-member Senate and a Legislative Assembly of 32 members. The Senate was composed of representatives of the clergy, the nobility, the University, the Chamber of Commerce and the Trade Union Council. The members of the Legislative Assembly and seven members of the Senate were elected by adult males, subject to certain minimal property or educational restrictions.

The 1921 Constitution was suspended in 1930 and again in 1933, and finally revoked in 1936. In spite of a new constitution in 1939, the islands remained effectively under Governor's rule until representative government was restored after the war. The 1947 Constitution again provided dyarchy, but it did not resurrect the cumbersome Senate. The new Legislative Assembly consisted of forty members elected by universal suffrage from eight electoral districts. In 1958, the government resigned following the collapse of talks with Britain over a proposal to 'integrate' Malta more closely with the United Kingdom. As the leader of the opposition refused to form a new government, the Governor suspended and then revoked the constitution.

I did the fieldwork on which this study is based at this period in Malta's constitutional history. A new constitution was promulgated late in 1961, and elections took place in February 1962. In place of dyarchy, it provided for 'concurrent powers' on foreign affairs and defence to be held by the Malta Government and a United Kingdom Commissioner.

The first Maltese political parties were born out of the controversy over language which followed the publication in 1880 of the Keenan report on education. This recommended that English should be taught in place of Italian in the primary schools, although students might later take Italian as an elective subject. In the Lyceum and the University, except for the Faculty of Theology, all work was to be done in English. These recommendations, which the government tried for many years to implement, weakened the dominant position which Italian had enjoyed in the educational system. As Italian was the language of the law courts, the clergy and the University, it was something of a class symbol. Most of the educated classes, and especially the lawyers and priests, strenuously resisted the move to downgrade it in favour of English. Many of the refugees from the Italian wars, who came to Malta after 1850, gave encouragement to the partisans of Italian. The Italian movement also whipped up considerable support amongst the clergy and their parishioners by declaring that English would certainly bring with it increased Protestant influences.

The dispute thus created interest groups which were to dominate Maltese politics for the next fifty years. On one side was the pro-English, or *riformista*, party led first by Sigismondo Savona, later the Director of Education, and subsequently by Count (later Lord) Gerald Strickland. This party, which generally supported government policy, favoured close cultural and political ties with Britain. By the 1920's, it became known as the Constitutional Party. Its successor, the Progressive Constitutional Party, is led by Strickland's daughter, Miss Mabel Strickland.

The *anti-riformista* or pro-Italian party was led by Dr. Fortunato Mizzi and later by his son, Dr. Enrico Mizzi. The Nationalist Party eventually emerged out of this group, and today, although the language issue is quite dead, it is still one of the two major political parties. Both parties campaigned for support in the villages and thus, for the first time, forcefully presented national political issues to the masses. The pro-Italian group came to dominate the elected members, and blocked the affairs of government to such an extent that Britain re-established the official majority.

Britain did not succeed until many years later in implementing the recommendations of the Keenan Report. The language of instruction in the primary schools remained English or Italian, at the option of a student's parents – the so-called 'pari-passu' system. In 1921, Britain attempted to remove language from the political arena by stipulating in the new constitution 'that nothing shall be done by way of legislation or administration which shall diminish or detract from the position of English as an official language or to reduce its use in education or in the public service.'[1]

For the first six years after the 1921 Constitution was promulgated, the government was in the hands of the political groups which eventually merged into the Nationalist Party: Monsignor Panzavecchia's 'Unione Maltese' and the 'Partito Democratico Nazionalista' led by Enrico Mizzi. The newly-formed Labour Party at first supported the Nationalists, but later became a firm ally of Strickland's Constitutional Party. Monsignor Michael Gonzi, now Archbishop of Malta, was a representative of the Labour Party until he became Bishop of Gozo in 1924. During this early period, the only serious political skirmish occurred, not surprisingly, over the 1923 Pari-Passu Bill by which the Nationalists introduced both English and Italian as compulsory subjects in the elementary schools. Strickland attacked the bill on the ground that it made no provision to teach Maltese, the language of the masses. He maintained that without a firm knowledge of their own language, children could never learn two foreign languages at the same time. Although the British at first declared that this act was contrary to the spirit of the constitution, it was allowed to become law.

The Constitutional Party, supported by the Labour Party, won the 1927 general elections, and Strickland became Prime Minister. The elections, however, were marred by an incident which embittered the relations between Strickland's supporters and their opponents. On the day before the election, the Nationalists circulated thousands of copies of a perjured affidavit which declared that Strickland was a Freemason. Although the perjurer, a

[1] Section 57.

notorious criminal whom the Nationalists hid until after the elections, was later convicted, the accusation jarred the solidly Catholic electorate and undoubtedly cost Strickland many votes.

In the years that followed this election, Malta was torn by an unprecedented political struggle between the Strickland Government and the Church. Since this dispute in many ways foreshadowed the present conflict between the Church and the Malta Labour Party, it is worth while to examine it in some detail.

While Strickland was the leader of the opposition, he made frequent attacks, both from the floor and through his newspapers, on the priests sitting in the Assembly. He maintained that the clergy should not take part in politics. In doing this he made many enemies, for his attacks were often bitter and insulting. For example, he once offered a cash prize to the person who gave him the best reason for having the Bishop of Gozo removed from office. On another occasion, he announced that for a small sum of money, even a horse could become a Papal Marquis.

Relations between Strickland and the Church, already strained, deteriorated rapidly after he became Prime Minister. When the two monsignori who represented the Archbishop in the Senate voted against his first budget, he considered that the Church had declared war on him. This was followed by a public demonstration against the Archbishop. At the same time, Strickland also launched a blistering attack through his newspapers on the two clerical Senators. Following this, there was a whole series of petty disputes which culminated in the famous Father Carta case.

Father Carta, a Sardinian monk, had been sent to Malta by the Superior General of the Franciscan Conventuals to resolve a disciplinary problem in one of the Order's Maltese convents. He soon discovered that a certain Maltese monk, Father Guido Micallef, was one of the principal trouble-makers, and arranged for his transfer to the Order's house in Liverpool. At this point Strickland intervened. He asserted that Father Micallef was being exiled because he had supported the Constitutional Party in the 1927 elections, and refused to issue the necessary exit permit. The Church was furious at this interference in what it regarded as its internal affairs. In the wrangle which followed, both the Governor and the Archbishop became involved, Father Micallef was expelled from the Order and defrocked, and the Cabinet asked the Governor to petition the Holy See to investigate the incident.

A Papal Delegate visited Malta and concluded that the differences between the government and the Church could best be settled by means of a concordat. During most of the year following the Papal Delegate's visit, Britain tried unsuccessfully to negotiate a concordat and to get the Holy See to forbid the Maltese clergy to take part in the general elections scheduled for May 1930. The Vatican, however, declared that Strickland was not *persona grata* and that as long as he remained in power, a concordat was not possible.

In Malta, the relations between the Strickland Government and the Church went from bad to worse. In April 1930, two Constitutional Party Ministers gathered many sworn statements that Monsignor Gonzi, the Bishop of Gozo, had instructed priests to preach against the Constitutional Party and to refuse absolution to its supporters. This inquiry greatly angered the Church. On the first of May, the Archbishop and the Bishop of Gozo issued a joint pastoral which forbade people to vote for Strickland or those candidates who supported him. In view of the spiritual sanctions that threatened people who voted for the candidates of one of the two major parties, Britain had no option but to cancel the elections. It subsequently suspended the constitution, but kept the Strickland ministers on as advisers.

A Royal Commission went to Malta to investigate the trouble. Following its report, Britain restored the constitution and abolished the teaching of Italian in primary schools. In June 1932 the Nationalists defeated Strickland and his supporters in a bitterly contested election in which 96 per cent of the electorate voted. However, their period in office was very brief. The Governor dismissed them in November 1933 for deliberately evading the constitutional provisions regarding language, for they had set about to re-establish the primacy of Italian in the educational system and the civil service. Once again the administration of the islands became the responsibility of the Governor.

During the fourteen years of Governor's rule which followed, the deep wounds caused by the long, harsh political conflict slowly healed. The first Italian bombs of the war finally killed the language dispute. The united defence effort and the common suffering caused by the prolonged bombardment further helped to reunite political rivals and suppress parochial quarrels. Britain awarded the people of Malta and Gozo the George Cross for their heroism, and after the war restored representative government.

In the first election under the new constitution, the people voted overwhelmingly for the Labour Party, then led by Dr. Paul Boffa. But in 1949 a disagreement between Dr. Boffa and his Minister of Public Works and Reconstruction, Mr. Dom Mintoff, split the party. The Nationalists, with the support of Dr. Boffa's new Workers' Party, formed the next few governments. Dom Mintoff's Malta Labour Party gradually swallowed the Workers' Party and finally defeated the Nationalists in the 1955 general election.

There was almost constant friction between the Church and the Mintoff Government during the three years it was in office. From the outset, Mintoff showed himself reluctant to submit to the authority of the Church. His refusal to pay the traditional call on the Archbishop, Monsignor Gonzi, when he took office was symbolic of this independence. Many incidents contributed to the disagreement between the two, which grew more intense as both became more outspoken in their criticism of each other. Perhaps the most serious clash occurred over the Archbishop's stand on the Government's proposal to link Malta more closely with Britain. On the eve of a referendum concerning this proposal, Monsignor Gonzi made a broadcast in which he said that he could not support the integration proposal because Mintoff had failed (whether by design or circumstance is an open question) to secure adequate guarantees from Britain to protect the position of the Roman Catholic religion. In spite of this, the electorate supported Mintoff's proposal; but relations between the Labour Party and the Archbishop remained strained.

Then, shortly before he resigned, Mintoff sparked off a sharp dispute with the Church by hanging in the National Museum a painting taken from St. John's Co-Cathedral. Originally, the government had sent the painting, a Caravaggio, to Italy to be restored. But the government seized it when it returned and declared that since the Co-Cathedral was government property, the painting was a national treasure that should be properly cared for and displayed to the public. In the course of the acrimonious dispute which followed, Mintoff, who had appealed the matter to the Vatican, was ordered by the Holy See to return the painting. He finally returned it on the night before he resigned.

The relations between the Labour Party and the Church continued to deteriorate after the resignation; finally, in 1961, they gave way to open hostility. Both sides abused each other in the course of the election campaign. On 9th April the Church placed Mintoff and many of the Labour leaders under an interdict for their disrespect to the Bishop. A little over a month later, the Bishops issued a circular condemning the Labour papers. These sanctions intensified the conflict. Finally, just six weeks before the election, the Church, through the Diocesan Joint Council of Catholic Lay Associations, launched a massive campaign to persuade the people to vote against the Labour Party. The campaign was successful: the parties which the Church supported defeated the Labour Party at the polls, and the Nationalist Party took office.

The reader will have noted the similarity between the course of the conflicts of Strickland and Mintoff with the Church. Both took place after relatively long (for Malta) periods of representative government. Both involved a series of rather petty disputes which became progressively more bitter and divided the country. Both culminated in the Church imposing sanctions which ultimately led to the electoral defeat of its opponents. In each case, approximately one-third of the population chose to face Church sanctions rather than abandon its political leaders. Most of the actual incidents which provoked the disputes were quite out of proportion to the conflict they created. To my mind, these incidents were symptomatic of the inherent conflict between an elected government and a Church which has long exercised great authority in both secular and religious spheres.

It is not my intention to make a detailed analysis here of the complex causes underlying the present conflict between the Malta Labour Party and the Church. At this point it is sufficient to know that the dispute exists. In later chapters I shall be concerned with tracing its effects on the social organization of the villages. In the course of this study, it will also become apparent that there are conflicts between secular and religious interests in the villages which are quite unrelated to national political issues.

CHAPTER II

The National Organizations: State, Church and Political Party

Generally speaking, the activities of government are carried out by a number of departments and boards, each of which is under the control of a director or chairman. Each of these, in turn, is usually responsible to an elected Cabinet Minister. But under the interim constitutional arrangements which followed the resignation from office of the Labour Party in 1958, Department Heads were responsible to a British Chief Secretary and his assistants. Under each Department Head are ranked the various grades of civil servants. These run from the Executive and Clerical Officers through non-pensionable clerk-typists, fatiguemen and industrial labourers. Altogether, some 17,000 persons work for the government. They represent 19 per cent of the total labour force. This makes the Malta Government the largest employer on the islands. Entrance to all but the lowest grades, and promotion between the principal grades within the civil service, are by means of open competitive examinations.

Malta's small size has facilitated the centralized administration required of an island fortress. As already observed, there are no councillors, headmen or mayors, either elected or hereditary, to represent the interests of the villagers to the government or convey the wishes and commands of government to the people. Virtually all the machinery and personnel of government are located in Valletta. Only the police represent government authority in all villages. There are government elementary schools for boys and girls in all villages and almost all hamlets. Now most villages also have a dispensary which is open for a few hours a day under the supervision of a government District Medical Officer and a nurse. There are a few regional post offices and branches of the Department of Emigration, Welfare and Labour. All other public services, such as street sanitation, sewerage (where it exists), water, electricity, repair of roads and so on, which in many countries are carried out by village or municipal authorities, are in Malta centrally administered from Valletta.

Gozo provides in some respects an exception to this picture. Though Gozo is administratively and economically dependent upon Malta, it has had for many years a certain measure of autonomy under a separate Commissioner. This appointment is dictated by the island's distance from Valletta in time and space. This isolation has not surprisingly resulted in a widely held belief that the Maltese administration, in which, incidentally, a large number of Gozitans have always held important posts, has systematically neglected Gozo. That there is a certain justification for this belief can be seen by anyone who compares the condition of the roads and the extension of street lighting, water and drainage in the two islands.

Partly to still for ever complaints about neglect, and partly as an experiment with a concept of local government new to Malta, the Gozo Civic Council was established in the summer of 1961. Each village in Gozo now has an elected committee of six councillors, one of whom represents the village on the Civic Council. The Council has the responsibility for the maintenance of roads, government buildings, cemeteries and public gardens, village dispensaries and the museum and public library. It can also construct new roads and extend drainage, water and street lighting. To finance its work the Council receives the revenue from local taxes and from certain government property in Gozo. It also has the power to levy rates, but as all councillors made solemn promises to their constituents that they would not do so, this additional source of revenue must be discounted for the time being.

II

The Maltese Islands form a single province of the Catholic Church. This province is divided into the Archdiocese of Malta and the Diocese of Gozo, which includes the small island of Comino. The Bishop of Gozo is suffragan to the Archbishop of Malta. As the senior or Metropolitan Bishop, the Archbishop has certain privileges and rights over his suffragan. These include the right to visit his suffragan's diocese (with Papal authority), should the latter neglect to do so; the right to appoint a temporary vicar on the decease of the Bishop of Gozo, if the Cathedral Chapter of the latter's diocese fails to appoint one within eight days; and the right to wear the insignia of his office which mark his superior dignity (the *pallium* and the double cross), throughout his province. Moreover, the Archbishop's court functions as a court of appeal for cases heard in the court of the Bishop of Gozo. In all other matters, however, the Bishop of Gozo has the same rights as the Archbishop. These include the right to make certain rules and dispensations for his diocese, to inflict penalties, interdictions and excommunication; and to determine who may be admitted to the priesthood.[1]

Each Bishop is assisted by a number of advisers, who also run the Curia, or administrative headquarters of the diocese. In the Archdiocese of Malta the Curia is under the charge of the Vicar General, who has the title of Titular Bishop. These advisers are for the most part Monsignori, or Canons, of the Cathedral Chapter. The Cathedral Chapter is composed of the priests attached to a cathedral church who advise the Bishop, arrange for a more solemn celebration of divine worship, and, when the See is vacant, provide for the government of the diocese. Though the Archdiocese of Malta has both a Cathedral in Mdina, and a Co-Cathedral in Valletta, there is only one Chapter.

In addition to the Cathedral Chapters in Malta and Gozo, there are also a number of Collegiate churches. The clergy of a Collegiate Church form a Collegiate Chapter, and have the title of Canons. They perform no special duties in the diocese. The title of 'Collegiate' is an honour which can only be bestowed upon a church with Papal sanction. There are Collegiate Chapters in Senglea, Vittoriosa, Cospicua, Rabat, Birkirkara and Valletta in Malta, and in Għarb, Nadur and Xagħra in Gozo.

The Archdiocese of Malta and the Diocese of Gozo are divided into 48 and 15 parishes respectively. A parish is the basic social and territorial unit of the Church. Every village in Malta and Gozo is a separate parish, though some towns are divided into two or more parishes. The limits of a parish are fixed by the Bishop. They often extend several miles beyond the compact villages that are so characteristic of the Maltese countryside. In most rural parishes there are also a few scattered farmsteads. The occupants of these isolated farms normally have houses in the village, to which they

[1] Cf. William E. Addis and others, 'Archbishop', *A Catholic Dictionary* (16th ed. rev.; London, Kegan Paul, Ltd., 1960), pp. 44 f.

move for religious feasts and family celebrations. Sometimes a number of these farms are clustered around a chapel or small church dependent upon the parish church. In time, these hamlets may disappear; historical sources cite many which have long since vanished.[1] On the other hand, a hamlet may grow to the point where its inhabitants can afford to build a larger church and in other ways successfully press their claim to become a separate parish. Most rural parishes in Malta and Gozo have come into being in this way. Some towns have been divided into two or more parishes for administrative reasons. In Malta, Qormi and Valletta are each divided into two parishes, and Sliema into three. Rabat in Gozo is currently being divided into two parishes. But because of fierce rivalry between the residents of the territories concerned, the exact boundary line is disputed and the territorial division will probably take another generation to complete.

The parish priest, who in all but the smallest parishes is assisted by a curate or more, is responsible to the Church for the care of the souls of all Catholics resident in his parish. Except where foreign service personnel live with their families – notably in Rabat, Naxxar, Mosta, St. Paul's Bay, Luqa and Birżebbuġa – all villagers are Catholic, and are thus the priest's parishioners. These parishioners also form part of the corporate body of the Church.

The clergy in Malta, as in all other Catholic countries, are divided into two main groups: the secular or diocesan clergy, and the regular clergy. Diocesan priests are trained in the Bishop's Seminary and are directly subject to the authority of the Bishop. A further distinction is made between those diocesan priests whose families or patrons have been able to provide them with a bene-fice – either property or cash deposited at the Curia bank – yielding a minimum of £10 annually, and those who have received their benefices from their Bishop. After the first five years the former, who are by far the most numerous, are free to serve where they wish. The latter always remain at the service of their Bishop. Most parishes are run by diocesan priests, and the clergy resident in the villages belong to this group. The friars and monks of the regular clergy are members of religious orders. They have been trained in the seminaries and houses of their particular orders.

[1] An interesting study of villages which have disappeared is given in M. Richardson, *Aspects of the Demography of Modern Malta* (Unpublished Ph.D. dissertation, University of Durham, 1960), pp. 243 ff.

They must live together in specially designated premises under the discipline of their order, and they are subject to the authority of their provincial or superior. As we shall see, the position that the clergy occupy in society and the nature of their work is to a very considerable extent determined by their sheer numbers. In 1957 there were 1,229 diocesan priests, friars and monks and 1,588 nuns in Malta and Gozo.[1] In addition to these, in 1958 there were approximately 220 friars and monks and 200 nuns studying abroad or working as missionaries or chaplains to communities of migrants.[2]

There are a number of associations which occupy important positions in the structure of both the diocese and its constituent parishes. At the diocesan level the most important of these are the College of Archpriests and Parish Priests, which acts as a pressure group in the interest of its members; the Cana Movement, which runs courses for engaged couples, a marriage advisory council and a clinic; and the Social Action Movement, which is trying to establish trade unions. There is also the Diocesan Junta, or Diocesan Council of Catholic Lay Organizations. This body, on which most of the diocesan and parochial societies are represented, is an important pressure group. As already noted, it played a leading part in bringing about the defeat of the Malta Labour Party in the 1962 elections.

Many associations, though organized at the diocesan level, have semi-autonomous branches at the parish level. These can be roughly divided into the lay apostolate associations and the devotional societies. The lay apostolate groups have been organized so that 'the Church will be able to exercise its direct and indirect action in all the fields: religious, cultural, technical, family, workers' movements and others.'[3] These societies are usually divided by age and sex, and except for the Society of Christian Doctrine, all are run by village priests who are responsible to the parish priest. These chaplains and the lay leaders generally work out an active programme of lectures, good works and outings. Many of them take part in religious processions and, in general, support the work of the parish priest. Together with the clergy,

---

[1] *1957 Census of the Maltese Islands: Report on Economic Activities* (Valletta, Central Office of Statistics, 1958), p. 45.
[2] Charles G. Vella, ed., *The Catholic Directory of Malta and Gozo* (Valletta, Archbishop's Palace, 1958), pp. 273–308.
[3] François H. Houtart, *in* Vella, p. 311.

3

they provide the organized opposition of the Church to the Malta Labour Party.

The most active of these societies are the Catholic Action, the Young Christian Workers, the Legion of Mary and the Sodality of Our Lady. Since the aims of these groups are all very much alike, there is a certain amount of rivalry between them for members and for recognition as the most active society in the parish. The position of Catholic Action as the leading lay apostolate society is being challenged by the Legion of Mary and the Young Christian Workers, whose militant opposition to the Labour Party has generated much publicity.

The Jesuits introduced the Young Christian Workers movement in 1945. Its members today, however, are for the most part young unmarried white-collar workers. This is an occupational class which does not generally support the Labour Party. The male sections of Catholic Action and the Young Christian Workers usually have their own premises, with facilities for table tennis and billiards, and sometimes a bar and library.

In all villages, the Church societies with the greatest membership are those which cater for women and girls. Few of these groups have premises of their own; they usually meet, separately, several times a week in one of the smaller chapels that are to be found in all villages. There the members say prayers and listen to lectures and sermons from their chaplains. They also teach catechism, look after church vestments, visit the sick and in general perform useful work for the parish priest and the clergy. Many village girls are members of one or other of these groups until they get married. For, quite apart from the religious benefits they may derive, they find in them a certain organized companionship, especially after they leave school.

The strictest and one of the oldest of the lay apostolate groups is the Society of Christian Doctrine. It is more commonly referred to as *tal-muzew* or MUSEUM (Magister Utinam Sequatur Evangelium Universus Mundus). A Maltese priest founded the society in 1907 with the object of giving a deep religious formation to its members through a life of prayer and instruction. Although MUSEUM members live at home and work alongside others, they may not smoke, attend any kind of public entertainment, cultivate friendships with non-members, read secular newspapers or join other associations. Moreover, the men are required to cut their hair short, are not allowed to wear neckties, and must wear jackets in public. Female members are obliged to wear the traditional Maltese *ghonnella* (also *faldetta*). This is a black silk cowl which renders the wearer completely shapeless. Finally, all members are tied by a promise of celibacy. Since members usually enter the society as children, and work up through grades until they become full members, this promise ensures that all are either bachelors or spinsters.

The male and female sections are completely separate. Each meets daily under its respective superior in its own house. There the members hold devotional exercises, conduct study groups for adults and also teach catechism to the children. The superiors are normally elected for life; but if the members cannot agree, the national superior general, after consultation with the parish priest, appoints an acting superior, either from the village or from outside groups.

The society is somewhat unusual among village religious associations, since no member of the village clergy is directly involved in its activities, though priests are often invited in to give lectures. This relatively independent status, and the close contact that members maintain with their national headquarters, has led some parish priests to look upon it as a potential threat to their authority and consequently to oppose its establishment in their parishes. Thus, although the society has spread to 40 (83 per cent) of the Maltese parishes, it is only established in 6 (40 per cent) of those in Gozo, Malta's conservative sister island. In point of fact, wherever it has been established it has supported the authority of the parish priest, and its members are now among the staunchest opponents of the Labour Party.

In each parish there are usually several loosely organized groups such as the Association of Christian Mothers and the Holy Name Society which meet infrequently for special prayers and devotions.

Finally, there is at least one confraternity in each parish. A confraternity is a lay religious society which is dedicated to a particular saint and offers Masses for dead members. These societies, called *fratellanzi*, are the oldest associations in Malta, and many date back to the Middle Ages. Formerly certain confraternities in the larger villages and towns acted as trade guilds; others only enrolled persons of the highest socio-economic class. Both men and women may enrol, as members; but only men may wear the distinctive habit of the confraternity in processions, in which the *fratelli* play an important part. Entrance to a confraternity is by means of a short religious ceremony and the payment of a small fee. This entitles the newly professed member to share in the indulgences, privileges and spiritual favours which have accrued to the society.

Every confraternity is established independently in each parish, and has nothing to do with confraternities of the same name in other villages. Before the band clubs were established, confraternities were the only formally constituted associations in rural parishes. Their officers enjoyed considerable prestige, and had a voice in village affairs. But today the members seldom meet as a group and most confraternities have no premises of their own, though they generally have an altar in the parish church. Aside from the dozen or two who take part in all the parish processions, members take no part in any activity. A few confraternities which own property are a notable exception. Their officers meet occasionally to discuss the business affairs of the confraternity, and the societies still play an active role in local affairs.

There are also a number of third orders. These societies are lay counterparts of certain religious orders. They are organized in much the same way as the confraternities. Members attend occasional spiritual exercises and have the right to take part in processions and to be buried in the habit of the order. Altogether there are 16 different confraternities and third orders. Among the most common are the confraternities of the Blessed Sacrament, which is established in all parishes, the Holy Rosary, Our Lady of Consolation (*Ta' Ċintura*), St. Joseph and the Third Orders of the Franciscans and the Carmelites.

All groups and individuals that are tied to the Church are ranked. Each parish, religious order and parish society has its fixed position in the overall order. The same applies to the clerics who constitute its personnel. Position in the hierarchy is determined by seniority of foundation in the case of parishes and associations – or date of ordination or appointment to present office, in the case of the clergy – in combination with certain marks of honour conferred by the Church authorities. Such honours carry with them a claim to higher precedence than seniority by itself would give. For example, any parish in which there is a Collegiate Chapter, or whose church has the title of Basilica, ranks higher than one

which does not have these honours. Other honours are the right
to perform rituals, indulgence to persons visiting the church, and
particular ecclesiastical offices. To a considerable extent these are
rewards for meritorious conduct, measured by contributions to
the decorations of the church, or the number of vocations, or
special devotions performed in a parish.

During certain religious processions and ceremonies this rank-
ing becomes an important determinant of the order in which the
participants take part. Formerly, during the annual St. Gregory
procession, virtually the entire hierarchy of Malta could be seen
lined up on the ground. But this procession of parishes was
abolished and the ceremony modified in 1927, among other
reasons because of a dispute between the Canons of Senglea and
Birkirkara over a question of precedence. But the St. Gregory
procession in Gozo is still held every March. Then it is possible
to see parish following parish in order of precedence, and the confraternities of each, in their turn, ranked according to their position in their own parish hierarchy. At the front of the procession
is the youngest parish, the one with the lowest rank. It is followed
by parishes in ascending order of seniority until the oldest
Collegiate Chapter. Then come the religious orders. These are
followed by the clergy of the Cathedral and the Monsignori of the
Cathedral Chapter. The celebrant or Bishop brings up the end of
the procession. This inverted order of precedence is an important
organizational principle which operates in the secular as well as
the religious sphere, and it is one of the basic causes of disputes
between villages and band clubs.

III

At present there are six political parties in Malta. Of these, only
three contested the 1955 elections: the Nationalist Party (NP), led
by Dr. Giorgio Borg Olivier; the Malta Labour Party (MLP),
whose leader is Dom Mintoff; and Miss Mabel Strickland's Progressive Constitutional Party (PCP). The election resulted in 23
seats for the MLP, 17 for the NP and none for the PCP. Three new
parties have emerged since the resignation from office of the MLP
in 1958: the Democratic Nationalist Party (DNP), led by Dr.
Herbert Ganado, split from the Nationalist Party; Anthony
Pellegrini, a former Secretary of the Labour Party, founded the

Christian Workers' Party (CWP); and Chev. George Ransley started up the Democratic Christian Party (DCP).

Of these six parties, only one, the Malta Labour Party, incorporates the villages on a permanent basis in its organizational framework. The other five parties are loosely organized. Their structure can be seen most clearly just before an election. At the top of each there is the party executive. Below that are the candidates from the electoral districts. (Under the 1947 Constitution there were eight electoral districts each returning five representatives; the 1961 Constitution increased the number to ten.) The candidates from the various electoral districts work out their campaign strategy with their national executives. Each candidate, in his turn, tries to appoint canvassers or agents in each important village in his district. Some canvassers are paid, and have represented other candidates and parties before. Thus at the village level it is pretty much every candidate for himself. This is particularly true when there are several candidates from a single party canvassing votes in the same village. If the party is successful, the chain from canvasser, through the local member of the Legislative Assembly (MLA), to Cabinet Minister, serves as a channel for requests and patronage. The party structure is thus strengthened and given a degree of permanence. But if the party is defeated or, if elected, it resigns, or the constitution is suspended, it ceases to be an operative organization at the village level. None of these parties have permanently organized village committees or clubs, though there are Nationalist Party clubs in a few towns. In the past, a few band clubs became identified with specific parties and served as local centres for the party. This often occurred when prominent band club members became successful party politicians. But the linkage between a village band club and a particular party was coincidental. Moreover, only rarely did all the members of such a band club support the political party with which its leaders were aligned. The above, in rather general terms, is a rough description of the structure of five of the six Maltese political parties in 1961. The Labour Party is the exception.

The Labour Party was the first to reorganize itself immediately after the war. During the period between 1949 and 1955, when the Nationalists and Dr. Boffa's Workers' Party carried on a coalition government, Dom Mintoff further reorganized and strengthened the Malta Labour Party. Its structure was greatly reinforced during the three years following 1955 when it formed the government. Since then it has been streamlined and hardened by the Party's almost constant struggle with the Church. Frequent meetings now keep the rank and file in close touch with the national leaders. The Party's newspaper, which became a daily shortly after Mintoff resigned in 1958, disseminates propaganda and news of Labour activities as well as international news, and so provides the leaders with an important contact with members.

The MLP is now organized in three tiers: at the national level, at the level of the electoral district, and at the village level. The structure of the MLP, unlike that of its rivals, rests very firmly on its village level organization. Virtually every village in Malta has its own Local Committee, the members of which are elected annually by the formal, dues-paying members among the MLP supporters in the village. In most villages there is also a Party club, of which the Local Committee members are the officers. The Labour Club, which is usually equipped with a bar, a television set and a billiards table, serves as the social centre for the MLP group in the village. Its frequent activities keep the supporters united, as do the attacks of their enemies. The Club has become something of a refuge for MLP supporters who are now cut off from many village activities by the stigma which the Church has attached to them. A number of Local Committees have organized sub-committees for women and children.

Every Local Committee in each electoral district elects one member to sit on the District Committee. This Committee acts as a clearing house for propaganda and electoral tactics. During the three years that the Party formed the government, the District Committees were also points at which district-wide complaints, patronage and public works were discussed with the district MLA's.

At the apex of this pyramid is the National Executive of the Malta Labour Party. This is composed of representatives from all the District Committees, from the Parliamentary group and from the Labour League of Youth. The Party officers and additional members of the Executives are elected at an annual General Conference. All electoral candidates and major policy decisions are confirmed there. Conference delegates are representatives of the Local Committees of each village and town.

During the period the MLP was in power, the Local Committees were transformed from propaganda and social centres into instruments of government. As the village branches of the party in power, they represented government in the eyes of the people, if not the civil servants. They transmitted and explained the policy of the administration and they channelled requests to the appropriate authorities. Ministers made use of the Local Committees for business at the village level, since the Committees generally provided their only direct contact with the villages.

IV

The State, the Church and the political parties are thus the national organizations which affect the lives of the people at the village level. The State is highly centralized, and has no political representatives in the villages. In contrast to the State, the Church has its official representatives in every village and hamlet. They are firmly controlled from above. The structure of the Malta Labour Party also rests firmly on its village level organization. The differing structural frameworks of these organizations have a direct bearing on this study. While competition for power at the national level between the State, on the one hand, and the Church or political parties, on the other, can often lead to bitter disputes, such conflict rarely causes division at the village level. In contrast, disputes at the national level between the political parties, or between a political party and the Church are transmitted immediately through their respective structures to the level of the village. There they bring about a conflict of interest which reflects the struggle for power at the national level.

CHAPTER III

The Villages and Their Inhabitants

The villages with which this essay deals are the communities outside the densely populated built-up area which centres on Valletta. This area is contained in a rectangle formed by imaginary lines running from St. Julians' and Lija, and thence to Tarxien and Kalkara.[1] Many of these villages, however, are in reality rural towns with populations of up to 15,000, as in the case of Qormi. The Maltese do not distinguish linguistically between small villages and country towns, both are called 'villages' (*rhula*; sing. *rahal*). These are contrasted to *Il-Belt*, the City of Valletta, and its environs. Although I contrast town and country, it is worthwhile pointing once again to Malta's small size. No village in Malta is more than an hour's bus ride from Valletta, and Gozo is only thirty minutes by ferry from its larger sister island. Moreover, 'rival' villages are often no more than a few hundred yards apart.

I am here concerned with abstracting certain principles of social organization, and not with comparing the size and shape of residential groupings, although these two ends are obviously not completely unrelated. Consequently, the geographical limitations which I have placed upon this study are somewhat arbitrary. It is, perhaps, easier to think of the division between town and country as a continuum, with Valletta or Sliema at one end, and small villages such as Qrendi or Gharb at the other. Although much of the description and analysis which follows holds true for both town and village, I am here dealing specifically with the villages.

The separation between town and country corresponds to a rough division of economic and political power, for villagers look to the urban area for employment, income and patronage. First of all, the seat of government is in Valletta, and most of the senior civil servants live there or in Sliema, the sprawling residential suburb that has grown up opposite Valletta during the last 100 years. Secondly, almost all the professionals, wealthy business men,

---

[1] See the map of Malta and Gozo on page 2, above.

landlords and other important people who influence the affairs of the country live and work in the city or its suburbs. Finally, the greater part of the island's wage-earning population travels to work in this area.

Differences in language, dress and education set many of the villagers apart from their urban compatriots. That this should be so is not surprising, for the inhabitants of the city have been in contact with the country's foreign masters for many centuries. The Maltese upper classes, and those who aspire to be so considered, have studiously imitated the manners, speech and dress of these foreign residents. An English visitor early in the seventeenth century remarked on this contrast between the townsmen, who struck him as being 'altogether frenchified', and the countrymen, whom he described as 'half clad, and indeed a miserable people'.[1]

There is a noticeable difference between the heavy consonants and broad vowels of the uneducated countryman, and the English-accented Maltese of the inhabitants of Sliema, many of whose children speak more English than Maltese. There are also differences in vocabulary and inflection, for the language spoken in Valletta and the towns contains many more Italian and English words and expressions than the village Maltese. In fact, their preference for foreign words has given the inhabitants of Sliema the collective, and slightly derogatory, nickname of *tal-mama*, which derives from their habit of using the Italian word *mamma* (mother) instead of the Maltese *omm*. Village children, however, are now taught a standard Maltese at school, and they are urged to substitute this, *il-Malti bil-pulit*, for their local dialects.

The social and cultural differences between town and country have led to the creation of stereotypes. The typical townsman was often described to me by villagers as a white-collar worker who goes to cocktail parties, tries to look like an Englishman – pipe, tweeds and moustache – and speaks English to his children. The villager, on the other hand, is portrayed as an illiterate rustic who spends his money on wine and fireworks, without a thought for the future of his children. Both caricatures, of course, are gross exaggerations, but each, none the less, contains elements of truth. But many farmers and poor village labourers make great sacrifices in order to give their children an education beyond the elementary

[1] George Sandys, *A Relation of a Journey Begun A.D. 1610* (London, W. Barnett, 1615), p. 234.

level. There are also many village clerks and teachers who speak English to their children to help prepare them for school, for a sound command of English is a prerequisite to social advancement.

It is quite true that education has been given greater emphasis in the urban areas than in the villages; but the introduction of compulsory education between the ages of six and fourteen is rapidly closing this gap. The spread of education is reflected in the decline of illiteracy. In 1948, just two years after the introduction of compulsory education, 16 per cent of the population of Valletta and Sliema over fourteen years of age, and 47 per cent of the same age group in Gozo, were illiterate. By 1957, these figures had fallen to 9 per cent and 22 per cent respectively. During the same period, the national illiteracy rate declined from 37 per cent to 17 per cent.[1]

A number of other forces operate to reduce the social distance between town and country. The greater employment opportunities during and after the war, and the continuous improvement in public transport that allowed the villagers to take advantage of them, have placed an ever-increasing number of villagers alongside townsmen at desks and work benches. The war itself was a major force in the same direction, for British troops and people from the urban areas were evacuated to the country to escape the bombing attacks, and so shared the life of their rural neighbours. All learned a good deal from one another. It is not surprising, therefore, that many Maltese, especially in the villages, regard the last war as a social milestone, a dividing line between past dependence upon agriculture and present wage labour, between poverty and relative prosperity.

II

The inhabitants of the villages in Malta no longer derive their livelihood from agriculture, though this was the rule a century ago. Today most are semi-skilled and unskilled industrial labourers who work outside their villages for the Malta Government, the

[1] *Eleventh Census of the Maltese Islands, 1948* (Valletta, Progress Press), pp. 297 ff.; and *1957 Census of the Maltese Islands: Report on Population and Housing* (Valletta, Central Office of Statistics, 1958), pp. 41 ff. The two sets of figures are not quite comparable. Those for 1948 represent the total number of illiterates, while the 1957 figures show only the number of people who never attended school.

giant dockyard in Cospicua, or for one of the various British Service departments scattered over the island. Gozo is more dependent upon agriculture, but many Gozitan men work in Malta, returning to their families for the weekend. Though Maltese villages are populated mostly by industrial workers, they have nonetheless a decidedly rural atmosphere about them, for their inhabitants still have links with the agricultural economy of the past. Many retain a patch or two of land which they plant with potatoes or some other cash crop to supplement their wages, and virtually all keep chickens and rabbits to supply them with eggs and fresh meat for special celebrations.

TABLE I. Occupational Classes in Farruġ and Kortin[1]

(Expressed as percentages of the total male working population)

Occupational Class	Farruġ	Kortin	Islands
Professional and Clerical	4	7	15
Service and Skilled	39	52	55
Semi- and Unskilled	42	27	20
Agricultural	15	14	10
Totals	100	100	100

A hundred years ago, the inhabitants of Farruġ were mostly farmers, though many were also employed on a cottage-industry basis in the thriving cotton industry of the time. Today they are for the most part wage labourers. Of the total male working population, 42 per cent are employed as semi-skilled and unskilled labourers, 39 per cent work as skilled fitters and as service personnel (shopkeepers, drivers, policemen, etc.) and 15 per cent as farmers. Only 4 per cent are professionals and white-collar workers. Three-fourths travel outside the village to their places of employment, chiefly with the Malta Government and the British military departments.

The occupational structure of Kortin is much the same. The higher proportion of skilled and clerical workers is in part a reflection of its past importance as an administrative centre, for until early in this century it was the seat of the district court. Seven per cent of the men work in professional and white-collar

---

[1] The figures for Farruġ and Kortin are based on surveys I conducted, and the national figures on the *1957 Census: Report on Economic Activities*, pp. 45–55. The totals of the male working population in Farruġ, Kortin and the Maltese Islands are 296, 1,131 and 75,930 respectively.

occupations, 52 per cent are service personnel and skilled workers, 27 per cent are unskilled and semi-skilled labourers and 14 per cent are engaged in agriculture. Just over two-thirds of the total are employed outside the village. The majority of these, as in Farruġ, work in the Grand Harbour industrial area. Those who work in the village are for the most part self-employed. They are farmers, shopkeepers, blacksmiths and carpenters.

In Table No. 1 I have compared the various occupational classes in Kortin and Farruġ to each other and to the national figures.

III

Most villages look very much alike. Their magnificent baroque churches provide a startling contrast to the low, flat-roofed houses grouped tightly around them. As the parish church towers over the village, so it dominates it socially, for the church is in every sense the centre around which the life of the village revolves. In front of the church there is usually a large square, the *misraħ* or *pjazza*, which is the social centre of the village. Various village clubs and lay societies, as well as the police station, are situated on the *pjazza*, or just off it, as are the principal wine shops, the government dispensary and the finest houses of the village. As the square is usually the terminal point of the local bus line, it is the point at which most people enter and leave the village. It is also the stage on which the principal events of village life take place: the annual feast, or *festa*, of the patron saint, the many religious processions and the occasional political rallies. On Sundays, and especially during the long summer evenings, the square teems with groups of men, who sit about on steps and benches, talking and arguing for hours on end. During weekday mornings, it belongs to the old men of the village, now freed by government old age pensions from the backbreaking toil in the fields that was the lot of their forefathers.

Each village is first and foremost a community of neighbours. Even the smallest of them have distinct residential groups, the members of which are in closer contact with each other than with people living in other parts of the village. This is, of course, particularly true of the larger villages. But even in Farruġ, a village of about 1,400, the extremities of the village and the various streets and alleys form separate neighbourhoods. The many little shops scattered about the village permit the women to do most of their shopping near their own homes. Because of the long, hot summers when food spoils quickly, they shop separately for each meal. Their shopping trips begin on the way home from the early Mass, at about 4.30 or 5 o'clock in the morning, and continue until 7 or 8 o'clock in the evening. Thus, during the course of a day, a woman may make as many as a dozen trips to the shops as well as to the hawkers who pass through the neighbourhood. These trips are social occasions during which she comes in contact with friends and neighbours from all parts of the village, and in the process hears the village news.

The men are out of the village from 6 o'clock or so in the morning to about 2 o'clock in the afternoon in the summer, and in the winter from about 7 or 8 o'clock in the morning to 5 o'clock in the evening. But summer or winter, in the late afternoon and the early evening the men gather in the clubs, wine shops and cafés. Besides the clubs and important cafés in the square, which draw men from all over the village, there are many small neighbourhood wine shops. Most have a regular clientele of friends and neighbours who spend hours together talking, playing cards and drinking tea, soft drinks or wine. Many cafés also have television. Thus, though most inhabitants of a village are in fairly frequent contact with each other, the gossip groups of the women and the wine shops of the men form local social centres which help bind neighbours more closely to one another. These neighbourhoods develop a certain group loyalty.

It often happens that some of the neighbourhoods in a town or village are centred on small chapels. In times gone by there used to be a certain amount of good-natured competition between the youngsters of these districts over the festas of the patron saints of their respective chapels. But, except on rare occasions, this rivalry never threatened the unity of the village during the annual festa of the patron saint of the parish. Frequent removals from house to house within the village have usually helped to prevent the development of disruptive sectional loyalties.

Since each village is also a separate parish it is not possible to consider a village entirely as a secular community. Religion permeates the structure of Maltese society to an extent that makes it quite impossible to classify many institutions as either religious or secular. As a secular community, a village has no official leader, it

1. A Maltese Village

(Courtesy H.M.S. Falcon. Crown copyright reserved)

2. A village street

owns no land or other property in common and its inhabitants are rarely called upon or choose to work for a common end. At the same time, villagers are conscious of belonging to a distinct social entity which is distinguished from other villages by a collective nickname and a common sub-culture.

Many villages have a dialect quite distinct from that of their neighbours, which the inhabitants, even those who have learned to speak 'correctly' (bil-pulit), normally use to each other; although they will invariably address strangers in their school Maltese. There are also a number of minor variations of certain customs between villages or districts. These may include the way church bells are rung to announce a death or the way some aspects of the festas are organized. Finally, each village has its own very private body of gossip, stories, scandals and jokes, which makes up a part of its history and tradition that is not shared with outsiders.

As a congregation and a religious corporation, the village qua parish owns land and other property, including the parish church. It also has an appointed leader in the parish priest. The inhabitants of the village meet regularly for worship, to take part in religious processions and to carry out other devotional activities. Furthermore, they act together to celebrate the annual festa of the patron saint, who symbolizes the unity of the secular and religious aspects of the village, for he is patron of both village and parish.

A village can also be regarded as a moral community. That is, people who live there must conform to a certain code of conduct. While the community cannot enforce this code with the type of formal sanctions the police and the Church use to punish infractions of secular and religious laws, public opinion can, and does, exert great pressure for conformity. A person who flouts the canons of convention becomes the object of malicious gossip and, depending on the nature of the offence, he may also become the target of overt hostile action and have his house front splashed with paint, or his front door burned. The only way to escape from the sanctions of public opinion is to move to one of the urban areas or the expanding new suburbs, where licence can be relatively anonymous.

Members of a village thus share a common body of custom and tradition; they also display an intense loyalty to their place of birth. This sense of loyalty is strongest during the annual festa of the village, which draws in native sons and daughters from all over the country, and often from as far away as Canada and Australia. This loyalty is also evident at other times. Villagers like to think of themselves as a united body, and they take care to protect the appearance of unity before strangers. This is an attitude of which anyone studying the social history of a village becomes keenly aware. Strangers are thus treated with great reserve. The inhabitants of the smaller villages are well known for their reluctance to give any information about their neighbours to strangers. Inquiring visitors are often referred to the parish priest, who, as village spokesman, screens them and, if possible, deals with their questions. The reserve of a village *vis-à-vis* a stranger is considerably more than just an expression of village loyalty. Present also is the very real fear of vengeance should the answer to a stranger's question lead to some unpleasantness for a neighbour. Social relations in a small village are to a very considerable extent governed by the proverb 'Don't make an enemy of your neighbour' (*Taghmilx ghadu lil ġarek*).

In view of this loyalty, it is not surprising that people express their solidarity with their native village by opposition to other villages. A village's traditional rivals are usually those with which it has the most frequent contact. I was almost invariably warned by villagers that the inhabitants of the neighbouring village were a treacherous and savage lot. There are many tales of hostility between neighbouring villages, especially over the celebration of the annual festa, which I dare say have lost nothing in retelling. I was told a number of stories of how youths stampeded goats through their rivals' festa processions, and of expeditions which stole fireworks, attacked street decorations and performed other daring escapades. Although most of these adventures are said to have taken place many years ago, they are no more unusual than some of the incidents that I witnessed.

If the intense inter-village rivalry of former times has abated somewhat, it is probably because increased education and contact outside the villages have helped to break down ignorance and isolation. But this rivalry still lies dormant, and may flare up at the slightest provocation from a traditional rival; I have seen a number of fights over trivial incidents during festas and football matches. The number of police at village feasts and the quantity and density of the barbed-wire entanglements at the Schreiber

Stadium, where most village football matches are played, are in themselves evidence that fights during these occasions are the rule rather than the exception.

Although there is little formal contact between villages, there is a considerable amount of informal coming and going between their inhabitants. Most inter-village marriages are between partners from neighbouring villages, and the network of kin ties that these form helps to bind the villages of a district together. Inhabitants of neighbouring villages travel to and from work on the same buses, and see each other often at the annual feasts of the district. These multiple relations contribute to a certain district spirit. The most striking example is the unity of the Gozitans, although people from the south of Malta have something of the same spirit of belonging to a particular district. Nonetheless, the knowledge the inhabitants of the southern Maltese villages have of each other cannot be compared to that of the Gozitans, who, for the most part, not only recognize each other by face, name and nickname, but usually know a surprising (and often uncomfortable) amount of personal details about one another.

IV

A person becomes a member of a village by being born there, or marrying or moving into it. The administrative details connected with these acts are quite simple. Parents must register the birth of a child at the local police station, and the parish priest enters the child's name in his register when the baby is baptized, which usually takes place within a few days of its birth. If a man marries into a village, his name will be entered in the parish register, for under Church law the marriage must be performed by the parish priest of the bride, or his delegate. If the couple settles in the husband's village or in a strange village, their names will be recorded on the annual census there, the *status animarum*, which every parish priest prepares for his bishop. All changes of address are supposed to be given (but often are not) to the Rationing Office and, if the person is over twenty-one, to the Electoral Office. No other civil authorities are interested in a person's whereabouts.

In point of fact, however, most people live in the villages into which they were born. This is another respect in which the towns differ from the villages. While only about sixteen per cent of the adult population of an average Maltese village is not native born, approximately two-thirds of the adults residing in the urban and suburban areas were born outside the communities in which they now live (see Table 2 below).

There is no rule of village endogamy or exogamy, and a bride and groom are free to choose where they wish to live and set up their household. The choice of residence is normally governed by available housing, place of work and the relative strength of the bride's and groom's ties with their respective families and villages. But in case of a conflict of interest, a wife is expected to follow the wishes of her husband. If housing is available in both the village of the wife and that of her husband, and the husband's place of work is in neither, there is a tendency for the couple to live in the wife's village. The Maltese themselves acknowledge that, all other things being equal, the ties between a wife and her family are stronger than those between her husband and his kin.

Thus in Farruġ and Kortin, I found that approximately half the couples had married and settled within their respective villages. Less than one in twenty (4 per cent) of the couples were strangers who had moved there because of the shortage of housing in their own villages; and all of these had relatives already living in the two villages. The outsiders who married or moved into Farruġ and Kortin formed one-fifth (21 per cent) of the adult population, or about 10 per cent of the total population of each. In slightly over half (56 per cent) the marriages between people from these two villages and other villages, the husband settled in his wife's village. This is the general trend in Malta, where most men work outside their villages. In Gozo, where farming is the chief occupation, it is more usual for a woman to move to her husband's village, for that is his place of work. People from the towns who marry villagers are reluctant to move into the villages, and it is therefore fairly common to find villagers, especially women, moving to join their spouses in the towns.

The general principles regarding marriage residence are reflected in Table 2.

The number of outsiders resident in a village is an important factor governing the degree to which its inhabitants consider themselves a corporate group. As outsiders always retain strong links with their place of birth, the solidarity of a village is inversely proportional to the number of outsiders resident in it. Not only does loyalty to friends and relations in a man's village of birth often take precedence over new ties established by his marriage into a strange village, but it is not unusual for a man married into another village to continue to play an active part in the social life of his native village. Conversely, an outsider is seldom called upon or attempts to join the clubs and associations of his wife's village. Thus, only 3 per cent of the committee members of the fifteen band and social clubs in the sample villages I studied were outsiders, although about 18 per cent of the adult male population resident in these villages were born elsewhere. On the other hand, 5 per cent of the committee members were now living outside the villages in which they were born and hold office.

TABLE 2. Adults Born Outside their Place of Residence[1]

Place of Residence	Percentage born elsewhere	Males	Females
Urban/Suburban	66%	45%	55%
Maltese Villages	16	52	48
Gozitan Villages	15	39	61

Because of the many ties which bind people to their villages of birth, an adult who moves into his wife's village remains an outsider for many years. The village will probably not give him a distinctive village nickname, and he will be known simply as the husband of his wife, or perhaps by the name of his native village. Although the village may ignore his outside origin for much of the time, his place of birth is certain to be remembered and held against him by his enemies, should be become involved in a dispute. The children of an outsider, however, become full members of the village by virtue of their birth there, and their connection with the community through the family of their mother (or father). By the time his children begin to grow up and get married, the outsider is usually firmly established as a full member of the community.

[1] This table was compiled from data made available to me by the Principal Government Electoral Officer. It covers a random sample drawn from a sample of two suburban communities (Sliema and Balzan), seven Maltese villages (Żebbuġ, Għargħur, Gudja, Mosta, Qrendi, Dingli and Żurrieq) and three Gozitan villages (Qala, Xagħra and Għarb).

V

The Maltese have large families and reckon kin relationship equally through males and females. Each person is thus at the centre of a wide network of cognates and affines. All these relatives do not have equal importance; a person normally makes a distinction between his immediate family (*qraba tal-familja*), his close relatives (*qraba ta' ġewwa*) and his distant relatives (*qraba fil-boghod*). A man's immediate family consists of his parents and his siblings and their fiancées, wives and children. This set of relatives normally sees each other at least once a week, and would be invited for a baptismal or betrothal celebration. The close relatives usually include grandparents, parents' siblings and their wives and children – his first cousins. These relatives all expect to be invited to a wedding, if not to a baptism. If they live in different villages they will also exchange visits during their annual festas. Distant relatives include the siblings of grandparents and great-grandparents and their descendants. A person normally has no formal contact with this set, but he recognizes his relationship to them if it is known to him.

Upon marriage, a person extends the range of his immediate family to include the corresponding set of his spouse. He may meet more frequently with his wife's immediate family than with his own, especially if they live equidistant from both sets (or in his wife's village).

It should be noted, however, that these sets of kin are not fixed or bounded groups; a person is relatively free to invite whom he wishes to any given ceremony. Physical as well as genealogical distance combines with sentiment to determine the actual relatives who are placed in these rough categories by an individual. Thus a person may be on closer terms with a second cousin who lives next door than with a first cousin living in another village. Normally, however, certain relatives *expect* to be invited to particular ceremonies, and failure to do so leads to friction, or may be a reflection of an existing conflict. Thus, while a first cousin does not expect to be invited to a baptismal or betrothal party, he does expect an invitation to a wedding. A second cousin does not expect to be invited to either, although he often is. These sets of kin relations are thus flexible; long dormant links can be manipulated for special purposes, such as to arrange introductions to persons with political or economic influence. Once a kin relation-ship is made known, it establishes a special tie between the two parties, and preferential treatment often follows; for kin are expected to help each other.

The ties of kinship can also be extended artificially by asking non-kin to become godparents or marriage witnesses. Although parents normally choose persons to fill these offices from among their parents, uncles and aunts, thus reinforcing already existing kin ties, they quite often ask influential non-kin to perform this function. While the obligations created by godparenthood in Malta, as in Italy, are not as demanding as they are in Spain, and Spanish America,[1] the godparent (*parrinu*) is expected to favour his godchild (*filjozz*), if not the child's father.[2] Thus the institu-tion of godparenthood plays a part in the system of patronage. Influential persons, however, are more often asked to become marriage witnesses. This relationship is not enduring. When influential non-kin are asked to fill this office it is done as much to increase the prestige of the families of the couple getting married as it is to honour a patron.

There is constant informal contact between relatives living in the same village. These informal meetings strengthen kin ties and ensure that people have a wide knowledge of their kin. Thus a friend in Farruġ was able to name 49 households in the village (20 per cent of the total) whose members were descended from his father's six siblings. Although the spread of this old man's family was unusual, no one in the village did not have some relatives living there. The many cross-cutting bonds of kinship thus reinforce the multiplex ties created by neighbourhood, common culture and shared devotion to common symbols, and bind together the inhabitants of a village into the tightly united community which outsiders see.

[1] See Gallatin Anderson, *A Survey of Italian God-parenthood* (The Kroeber Anthropo-logical Society Papers, No. 15; Berkeley, 1956), J. A. Pitt-Rivers, *The People of the Sierra* (London, Weidenfeld and Nicolson, 1954), pp. 107 f.; and Sidney W. Mintz and Eric R. Wolf, 'An Analysis of Ritual Co-parenthood (Compadrazgo),' *Southwestern Journal of Anthropology*, VI (1950), 341–68.

[2] The reciprocal term *xbin* is used between a godparent and the father of his godchild. Friends and even strangers often use it to address one another; it is a way of reducing social distance and making possible a more intimate association. Michael Kenny in his book, *A Spanish Tapestry* (London, Cohen and West, 1961), p. 72, notes that this is also an Andalusian custom.

CHAPTER IV

The Basis of Leadership

The Maltese word for leader, *mexxej*, is seldom heard, and then only in reference to the leader of a political party. I once asked a parish priest who were the leaders of the village. He laughed and replied that there weren't any, because his parishioners did not like leaders. With the exception of the professionals and *il-puliti* from the towns, all the inhabitants of a village usually call one another by their Christian names and in general look upon each other as equals. This egalitarian outlook is compounded of many factors, of which the most important are similar occupation, standard of living and values, the detailed knowledge of each other's personal lives that comes with residence in a face-to-face community, and jealousy. Any person who attempts to lead or to try to start something new – such as a village playground – is derided. His true motive is seen as self aggrandizement and his enemies and envious neighbours are quick to point this out to others who may not have realized it. 'Envy follows the wise man like his shadow' (*L-ghira titrot wara l-gharef bhal dellu mieghu*), goes the Maltese proverb. Professionals and outsiders, especially if they are from the town, are occasionally able to start something new. Their social distance from most of the community protects them from the full impact of the envy and gossip which moulds so much of village life.

But in spite of the absence of official lay leaders and the conservative pressure of envy and gossip, there are a number of persons who have a greater say than others in the affairs of the community. They are able to do this by virtue of their social position, their occupation or office in one of the village associations or their influence with the parish priest. These persons, together with the parish priest, form the aggregate which can be said to run the affairs of the community. While there is no generic term for this aggregate, those who compose it are sometimes referred to as *il-kbarat*, 'the big ones', or more derogatively as *ir-rjus il-kbar*, 'the big heads'. But if asked, a person will often deny that such persons exist, and reply, 'Here we are all the same; we are all from the village'.

II

The authority of the State is represented by the police, who are formally responsible for law and order. Each village has a police station manned by a small contingent of constables under a sergeant. Several villages make up a police district under an inspector. In Malta most policemen live outside the villages in which they work. But it is usual for Gozitan constables stationed in Malta to be quartered in the police stations to which they are assigned.

In addition to their official duties of law enforcement, the police distribute voting certificates, help conduct censuses and give out the allotments of free food to old age pensioners and people on relief.[1] They also perform many favours for local residents. They help people fill out government forms, and occasionally allow the station telephone to be used for private calls. They are sometimes able to mediate in local disputes. Disputants very often report each other for insults, threats or some minor infraction of the law – throwing waste water and rubbish in the street is one of the most common – thus hoping to strangle their enemies in its due process. The police constable on duty is often able to reconcile the disputants and persuade them to withdraw the charges and counter-charges.

In general, the punitive role that the police are occasionally forced to play is offset by their role as distributors of government assistance and by their general helpfulness. District inspectors try to avoid personal relations with the people in their districts since they must prosecute all criminal cases, and personal ties might prove awkward. Sergeants and constables, on the other hand, normally maintain friendly social contact with the local inhabitants. They are often invited for drinks during feasts and weddings, and quite a number marry local girls. The Maltese police thus play

[1] The government has distributed surplus U.S. agricultural products to different groups of needy people since 1956. This food was first secured through the Co-operative for American Relief to Everywhere, Inc. (C.A.R.E., Inc.) and more recently through the Catholic Relief Services of America. The Department of Emigration, Labour and Social Welfare, not the police, selects the beneficiaries.

a very different role from that of their Spanish counterparts, the Civil Guard, whom Kenny describes as 'the traditional enemy of the peasants'.[1]

III

The very considerable authority of the Church in Malta is derived not from law, but from the loyalty of a people who fervently practise their religion. Until recently, there had never been a separation in their minds between Church and State, between the religious and secular elements in their daily lives. The Church, as we have already observed, has occupied this position for many centuries. Its power is bolstered by its considerable wealth, for in Malta the rich property and lands of the Church have not been expropriated by the State, as they have in so many other Catholic countries.[2]

As the official representative of the Church, the parish priest occupies a position of great importance in his community. He has authority in all religious matters affecting his parishioners. He ministers to their spiritual and often to their personal needs. He alone can arrange for the important ceremonies which mark the stages in their lives. These *rites de passage* include baptism, confirmation, marriage, death and burial. He also controls the many ritual activities of the village as a whole. These are the daily services of worship and the ceremonies, processions and feasts by which all Maltese, but above all the countrymen, regulate their days and mark the divisions of the year. Through his preaching and admonition he defines, interprets and enforces the moral code of the Church. He is also the official custodian of the richly decorated parish church.

Besides this dependence on the parish priest in the religious matters which are of such vital importance in the lives of a devoutly Catholic people, the country people have traditionally looked to him for assistance in many secular fields. Until only a few decades ago, he was often one of the few literate persons in his parish. As such he was frequently asked to read and write

[1] Op. cit., p. 48.
[2] Mitchell estimates that the Church owns 22 per cent of the agricultural land in Malta and 12 per cent in Gozo. See Peter K. Mitchell, *The Maltese Farm*, vol. II of *Studies in the Agrarian Geography of Malta* (mimeographed; Dept. of Geography, Durham Colleges in the University of Durham, 1959), p. 130.

letters. His high standing in the village, and his contacts with people of influence and power outside it, led people to turn to him for advice. He was asked to represent them in their relations with the outside world. In this capacity he served his parishioners as lawyer, banker and business adviser. He was also the traditional dispenser of charity.

The increasing literacy of the people and their ever-widening range of contacts outside the limits of the parish has somewhat reduced their dependence upon the parish priest. The State's recent involvement in welfare and charity has further weakened it. But if this dependence has been reduced, it has most certainly not been eliminated. Many still call on him to divide inheritances, to argue their claims against the government or to plead with prospective employers, and not a few expect him to be able to secure better roads, new schools, sewerage and playgrounds.

Thus the parish priest is the village's chief spokesman, and many still refer to him as *il-principal tar-rahal*, 'the head of the village'. The government has long recognized this, and makes use of him as a convenient contact with the people. Each Sunday morning, in addition to his own official announcements, the parish priest reads from the altar government notices advising the people of forthcoming elections, immunization campaigns, agricultural extension lectures and so on.

But if the parish priest performs numerous services for his parishioners, both individually and collectively, he has also the power to refuse them. The sanctions with which he can punish disobedience are considerable. They range from declining to write a good conduct certificate to denying absolution in confession. On the other hand, he has the power to give rewards for services rendered. Aside from doing favours for people who have helped him, he can appoint them to offices which confer prestige and authority and, in some cases, are also financially rewarding. All this serves to underline and reinforce his position as a leader in the community.

Parish priests are usually outsiders, but the rest of the village clergy are natives of the communities in which they live. Unlike Catholic priests in Britain or the United States, who live in presbyteries, the diocesan clergy of Malta and Gozo live at home with their relatives. This means that they remain in constant contact with the village. They are often called on to take part in family quarrels and village disputes, for their position in society makes them important allies. These demands frequently place them in the difficult position of having to choose between acting as an impartial servant of God and acting as a good son and loyal friend, who can only be impartial at the cost of making enemies of friends and family.

While parish priests, in all save the smallest parishes, usually receive an income sufficient for a reasonably comfortable life, few ordinary diocesan priests can live on their income as clerics. The average village priest gets only his daily Mass stipend of five shillings as compensation for his clerical services. If a priest is popular and gifted, he may be able to earn a bit extra by preaching, lecturing and taking part in religious functions in other parishes. Even so, most priests are forced to look to secular fields to be able to help support their parents and near relatives. Thus it is that most of the village clergy are part-time priests. That is, they spend most of the day away from their parish working at jobs that vary from farming to school teaching. Their pastoral work in their own parish is limited.

Of the eight priests born in Kortin and still living there, two are retired, one is the parish curate, two work outside the village as teachers and three are clerks with various diocesan bodies. In the evening most help the parish priest in church, teach catechism to the children and take charge of the various lay associations for which the parish priest has asked them to be responsible. In Farruġ there is only one local priest in the village. He teaches in the village's elementary school, and assists the parish priest in the evening, on Sundays and on feast days.

In almost every village there is an infants' school run by one of the female religious orders. The nuns are supported by donations of cash and produce from the local inhabitants. A few nuns earn something by doing elementary nursing among the sick of the community.

There are a number of other officers connected with the parish. These include the procurators (administrators) of the smaller churches and chapels, the sacristan, the choirmaster, the organist, the prefect of the altar boys, and so on. All have certain responsibilities delegated to them by the parish priest. In those villages where the celebration of the annual festa is organized by a committee, its members have the authority to command the financial and manpower resources of the community while they prepare for the feast. There are also the officers of the numerous religious associations.

In Farruġ, for example, there are two sections of the Catholic Action (youths and girls), a branch of the MUSEUM for men, and confraternities dedicated to the Blessed Sacrament, the Holy Rosary and St. Roque. There are considerably more in Kortin, which is a good bit larger. There are branches of MUSEUM for men and women, sections of Catholic Action for men, boys and girls, a section each of the Sodality of Our Lady and the Young Christian Workers, confraternities dedicated to the Blessed Sacrament, the Holy Rosary, St. Joseph and Our Lady of Sorrows, and sections of the Third Orders of St. Francis and Our Lady of Mount Carmel. There are also parish chapters of the Holy Name Society, the Christian Mothers Association and the Society of St. Vincent de Paul, a small, exclusive group which in Kortin raises about £50 a year to buy clothing and medicines for the poor of the parish.

Though the officers of the societies all have certain *ex officio* authority over the members, few are able to exercise authority in the village. Many are chosen by the parish priest to fill particular offices because of their pliability, religious conviction, or occupational status, rather than their qualities of leadership. But there are some officers who organize activities of concern to the entire community, and who consequently have a measure of authority in the wider community. These are the procurators of the parish confraternities and festas.

While the rector of a confraternity is its titular head, the procurator is the only officer who has any real authority. He keeps the registers of the society, recruits and enrols new members and often makes the arrangements for the funeral services of dead members. He also collects for and supervises the maintenance and decoration of the altar and statue of the society's patron saint. Furthermore, he makes all the arrangements for its annual festa. These may include collecting money, decorating the streets, booking brass bands and inviting priests to conduct the religious services and take part in the processions. His duties give him the authority to direct the action of others. He holds this authority, to be sure, in the name of and at the pleasure of the parish priest. The Church allows every procurator – whether of a confraternity, church, or festa – a three per cent commission on the entries in his financial registers to compensate him for his services.

Most of the procuratorships and offices in the associations connected with the Church are conferred upon members of the circle of persons who figuratively, and often physically, surround the parish priest. They become his favourites by doing some of the hundred and one odd jobs for which he depends on volunteers. These include running messages, carrying chairs, arranging meetings and decorating the streets for feasts and other important occasions, such as the visit of the Archbishop. Acceptance into the circle and the rewards meted out vary, of course, according to the capabilities of the individuals concerned, and the character of the parish priest. Advancement is most rapid and the rewards most interesting where the parish priest is open to influence, and the job-seeker has the qualities of leadership discussed below. But people are loath to see their parish priest delegate too much of his authority to their fellows. Those who pursue power in the community by attaching themselves to the parish priest often incur a good measure of hostility. Most frequently they are accused by the village gossips of lining their pockets with their neighbour's money.

The most important member of the circle surrounding the parish priest in Kortin is old Manwel, a retired school teacher. As procurator of the Confraternity of our Lady of Sorrows, he collects funds for and organizes the elaborate Good Friday procession. This is an event which attracts visitors from all over the island. He is also procurator of the Confraternity of St. Joseph, the village cemetery and the Mass legacies of the parish. He is one of the founders and a former vice-president and secretary of the Social Club, and a member of the Society of St. Vincent de Paul. Though no longer in the Band Club, he was once on its committee. For many years he was also on the committee which organized the annual festa. All these offices give him a greater voice in the administration of the parish and its ceremonial affairs than anyone except the parish priest.

IV

The officers of the secular associations in a village generally enjoy high standing and wield considerable influence. The secular associations, though they vary, generally include a men's social club (usually a brass band club), a political party committee or club and a sports club. In Farruġ, for instance, there are two band clubs – one of which is dedicated to St. Martin, the other to St. Roque – a football club and an active Labour Party committee; while Kortin has a band club, a social club, a Labour club, a football club and a troop of Boy Scouts. The term secular, used in this context, requires a few words of qualification. Although clubs and associations which I have called secular do not form part of the Church, this does not necessarily mean that they are opposed to it, or are cut off from it. Quite the contrary. Almost every club has a chaplain who serves as a link between it and the parish priest. Most clubs take part in certain religious functions, especially during the week preceding Easter. Moreover, many of the clubs have dedicated themselves to the Sacred Heart of Jesus and to the Immaculate Heart of Mary by means of special religious ceremonies. Often this dedication is renewed annually. Only the clubs of the Malta Labour Party do not have any linkage with the Church.

The band clubs are the most important secular societies. They are formally constituted associations with elected committees, premises of their own and a large body of dues-paying members drawn from all occupational and social classes. The first band clubs were established shortly after the middle of the last century in order to organize the external celebrations and provide music for the annual festas of village patron saints. The clubs multiplied rapidly, and soon became civic and social centres. They have broadened their scope to include dramatic groups, reading rooms and places where members can gamble out of sight of the watchful eyes of the law. Most clubs have large concert halls that can be used for wedding receptions. Today, each club usually has a well-stocked bar, a television set and a billiards table.

But a band club is more than just a social centre. As it usually plays an important part in organizing the external celebration of the annual festa, the men who run the club make decisions which affect all the inhabitants. Furthermore, the club often represents the community to the outside world. Not only is the club's brass band considered as the village's band when it plays at other festas, but the club also provides a welcome to important visitors from outside. Thus when the Governor or the Archbishop makes an official visit, he normally calls on the band clubs, where he is given a reception on behalf of the entire village.

The important officers of a band club are among the most influential people in the community, and are usually chosen from the village's leading citizens. The president is the figurehead of the club. He greets distinguished visitors and handles many of the ceremonial and business relations the club has with other groups within and outside the community. He also presides over committee meetings and over the annual election of new officers. The day-to-day running of the club is in the hands of the secretary, who is registered with the police as the club's official representative. Much of the success of the club depends upon his ability to run its social activities and administrative affairs. Other important committee members are the vice-president, the treasurer and the bandmaster. The latter is very often an outsider who comes to the village only for the weekly rehearsal of the band.

Though the formal authority of the committee members extends over the members of the association only while they are in the club, their position in the club occasionally gives them a voice in decisions which affect the entire community. This, in turn, gives them a measure of authority over persons who are not members of the club.

But not all villages have band clubs. The small villages of Għargħur, Dingli and Safi have not been able to afford the luxury of their own bands; though each has a social club that performs much the same function as a social and civic centre. A few villages, such as Kortin, have both social clubs and band clubs. But there are neither band clubs nor social clubs in the Maltese villages of Marsaskala, Marsaxlokk and Mġarr. In Gozo, only Rabat, Xewkija and Xagħra have band clubs. All the villages without clubs are fishing or agricultural communities. This may be because the men of these villages do not dispose of the leisure time in the evening necessary for a club to be a success: the farmers are too tired, and the fishermen are off tending their nets.

There are also political and football clubs in most Maltese villages. In Gozo there are a few football clubs, but no political clubs. These clubs are organized in much the same way as the band clubs, and corresponding office holders have similar functions and authority over their members. These offices, however, confer much less prestige. The football clubs, in particular, play only a small part in village affairs. The Malta Labour Party, as has already been noted, is the only political party which has clubs

3. Confraternity members resting during procession

4. Mace and canons of the Gozo Cathedral Chapter

at the village level. While there are Labour committees in almost all villages in Malta, not all of them have been successful in finding club premises. Where clubs have not been opened, the active members usually meet in a café or a private house.

The role of the Labour committee or club in the social life of a village is rather complex. The Labour club at all times is the centre of the local Labour supporters. During the past few years it has also been the centre of agitation against the established authority of the Church, especially in so far as it touches on secular matters. During the three years following 1955 when the Labour Government was in office, these village committees were backed by the government. Committee members thus wielded considerable power, for they provided a direct link with the established authority of the State at the national level. The same was true, but to a lesser extent, of the agents of the Nationalist Party during its period in government.

V

The qualities which the Maltese themselves consider important for a person to have in order to hold office are, of course, ideal ones. As such, they may not all be present in the same person. The leader of the St. Roque Band Club in Farruġ summed these up for me as responsibility, willingness to work, courage and social status (pożizzjoni). Responsibility and willingness to work are self-explanatory.

Courage is a necessary quality since any person in a position to exercise some control over the action of others (especially in a society which stresses equality) is bound to be criticized by those over whom he exercises it, as well as by those who envy his position. Courage may be based on a desire to acquire power, and insensitivity to or failure to perceive criticism, or on an idealism which places the ultimate ends above the criticism of the means employed to attain them. I have known various village leaders whose courage was based upon one or more of these attributes. I have also met people who resigned from their offices because their motivation or insensitivity was not sufficiently strong to prompt them to carry on in spite of criticism. A former secretary of the social club in Kortin once summed up the reasons for his resignation with the proverb, 'Unfortunate is the one who gets talked about' (*Miskin min jiġi f'ilsien in-nies*). This is especially true for those persons whose social position does not permit them to remain outside the circle in which criticism and gossip circulates. For these the esteem of neighbours is more important than office.

Social status is the fourth quality of leadership mentioned. High status is a desirable and, in some cases, necessary quality for the holders of certain offices. The president of a band club is required to act as its ambassador and to handle its external relations; a person with high status is an obvious asset. He can meet visiting dignitaries and perform the required speech making without embarrassment to the club. Thus the president and vice-president of the clubs have often been invited to fill those offices because of their high status. Some clubs create the office of honorary patron for benefactors who are willing to lend their names – and status – to the clubs, although they take no part or interest in their actual running.

High social position is also an asset to the office of treasurer; for at some time or another he is almost sure to be accused by the village gossips of putting his hand into the purse. Considerable social distance between him and his critics renders him less vulnerable to their comments. It also makes potential critics less vocal. People are often willing to concede integrity to their superiors which they deny to their equals.

The secretary of the club does not need high status to carry out his work successfully, although it is certainly an asset. But he must have at least one of the attributes of high status, namely education; for as administrator of the club he is required to do a great deal of paper work. On the other hand, occupying one of the important offices in itself confers prestige upon a person. Thus the secretary is accorded a higher social status that he would have if he did not occupy that position, assuming for a moment that he had no other attributes which would confer status upon him.

Two important attributes of status are education and occupation. Education is the key that unlocks the world of the printed word and frees people from dependence on patrons willing to interpret it. Education also leads to better employment opportunities. Since entrance to the civil service, the professions and many commercial concerns is by competitive examination, the Maltese attach great importance to formal education.

There is considerable difference in the social status ascribed to various jobs. Non-manual occupations have the highest status, manual occupations the lowest. The professionals – the priest, doctor, lawyer, chemist or teacher – are at the top; while the farmers are at the bottom. In many respects a government clerical officer is also at the other end of the scale from the farmer. The civil servant has a steady, relatively easy job with a good cash income and comfortable pension at the end. He also has ready access to influential persons in the government. His is a life of security and relative independence. The farmer, on the other hand, has been looked down on for centuries. He represents the traditional life of dependence: dependence upon the weather, the market, the *pitkal*, or middleman, for cash advances, the letter-writer and the patron through whom established authority has to be contacted. Education and wage labour have presented the farmer with a means of escape from that dependence and the exhausting labour in his rocky fields. Where he has had the opportunity, he has been quick to turn his back on the traditional occupation of his forefathers.

Wealth is another determinant of status. This is generally related to occupation. There has always been a considerable difference between the standard of living of the professionals and that of the average countryman. But until the past war, there was relatively little difference in the standard of living of most villagers. True, the more affluent lived in the large houses on the main square, and the poorer people lived in the alleys and streets remote from the square. Most people ate similar food, dressed alike and furnished their houses in the same way. But the increase in the level of wages, which followed the war, has changed that pattern. New houses, cars, fridges and transistor radios have become a tangible index of success and status. People are now being graded according to the number of these symbols they own.

Education, occupation and wealth are thus the chief criteria by which social position is differentiated. A person who has all these attributes has high status. But a person with high status is not necessarily a leader; for he may not possess the innate qualities required of a successful leader – courage, responsibility and willingness to work. Where a person has both high status and possesses these qualities – as well as ambition – he will undoubtedly be successful in the field of village politics. From there he can move into national politics.

Traditionally, age was an important determinant of status. Age meant wisdom, experience and position at the head of a large family. The deference accorded to age is preserved in the proverb 'Heed well the words of the elders' (*Kliem ix-xih żomm fih*). But in a society where teenage sons work as skilled labourers, clerks and teachers while their fathers still farm or dig ditches, and where schoolboys read letters, newspapers and voting instructions to their illiterate parents, the words of the elders are often not heard. The social and cultural gap between the old and the young is wider now than it has been for many generations. Today leadership in the villages is in relatively young hands. Old parish registers support the memories of the present generation of elders that this has not always been the case.

Village sons who are professionals often become presidents of their local band clubs. Very often they no longer live in their native villages. Most marry town-bred girls from professional families who do not wish to leave their urban surroundings and friends to live amongst people they regard as their inferiors in every sense. Though village-born professionals find it convenient for business purposes to live in the town, most lawyers continue to practise in their native villages. But when they continue to reside in their villages, even though their social life and many of their business interests are oriented away from the community, they normally enjoy great prestige. This works to enlarge their professional clientele. These assets can easily be converted into political support, and many village doctors and lawyers have gone successfully into politics.

Dr. Farrugia of Kortin, the town's only lawyer and its leading citizen, is a case in point. A native of Kortin, he is the son of old Manwel, the retired teacher who runs the Good Friday procession. Of a relatively modest background, he married the daughter of the former lawyer in the village, and took over the latter's large practice when he died. Past president of both the football and social clubs, a member of the St. Vincent de Paul Society, he has been president of the band club for many years. He is also a successful politician at the national level.

Frequently the government District Medical Officers are the only professionals resident in the villages in which they work.

Partly because of the temporary nature of their assignments, but also because they are usually city-bred, they generally keep themselves aloof from the people amongst whom they work. With but few exceptions, they take little or no part in the social life of the communities to which they are assigned. But they are nevertheless respected figures. Where they are tolerant of village customs, not too mercenary, and take a patronal interest in the personal problems of their clients, they will have, in addition to prestige, a large personal following. This has enabled a number of former District Medical Officers to stand successfully for elected office.

School teachers are another group of people with high prestige. Every village and almost every hamlet in Malta and Gozo now has a government school. Headmasters usually live outside the villages in which they work. They begin their careers in the small rural villages and move into the larger and more important schools as they gain experience and seniority. They are rarely in a village long enough to be asked to take part in its social life. Village-born teachers, on the other hand, normally teach in their home villages, where they often occupy important offices in the associations. But even where he no longer resides in his place of birth the teacher or headmaster, as a village son with high prestige, is often asked to take an active part in its social life. The president of the St. Roque Band Club in Farruġ, for example, is headmaster of the primary school in a neighbouring village, where he has lived since he married there more than forty years ago. He has been a member of the club's committee for most of that time, and its president for the last twenty years. Until two years ago he was also procurator of the Confraternity of St. Roque.

VI

The structure of authority in the villages of Malta and Gozo, because of the importance of offices and associations which are either focused on or articulated with the Church, bears a certain superficial resemblance to the civil/religious hierarchy which has been described in Mexican villages.[1] But it differs significantly; it is neither a hierarchy, nor is it formally related to the structure

[1] See, for instance, Fernando Camara, 'Religious and Political Oganization', in *Heritage of Conquest*, Sol Tax, ed. (Glencoe, The Free Press, 1952), *passim*.

of government. While the parish priest in Malta is the official village representative of the Church and has authority to act for it on most matters, the police represent only the law enforcement function of government; all other functions and services of government are administered from Valletta. In this respect the villages of Malta are unique.

On the other hand, there is a relation between social status and the functional requirements of the authority system. In any given community, the people with the highest status usually fill the most important offices, since such offices require the standing, skills and contacts which they possess. There is thus a rough grading of office holders in terms of their social status and the authority and prestige attached to their offices. Upward mobility through this structure is usually dependent upon factors such as education and occupation rather than on having held other, and less important, offices. Once a person has become the president of his local band club, in other words has attained the highest secular office in the village, and has a social status which commands respect outside, he may be elected to political office.

CHAPTER V

The Church and Village Politics

Most Maltese regulate their lives by the daily and monthly cycle of religious activities. The major divisions of the day are rung from the bells of the village church. They first ring the Paternoster half an hour before the first Mass. Then the Angelus bell rings a call to prayer at eight in the morning, at noon and at sunset. The final bell of the day is rung two or three hours after sunset, and is a brief request for the living to remember the dead in their prayers. The call of the Angelus is observed by many. When it is rung, work and conversation stop whether in a government office or a village café, men remove their hats, and someone among them leads them in a short prayer. In Gozo I have seen a busy square become suddenly silent and many people kneel in the street as the Ave Maria was rung at sunset. People also often kneel in the streets when the bells announce the elevation of the Host during a sung Mass, and during Benediction in the evening. And finally, late in the evening, clusters of relatives and neighbours can be seen sitting in their open doorways reciting the Rosary together before they go to bed.

Most girls and women and many boys and men attend one of the three or four daily Masses which are offered in all parish churches between four and seven in the morning. Virtually every one in the village attends one of the five or six Masses offered on Sundays. The few who do not attend are known to the village, and are the subject of gossip and other social pressure. Since the recent dispute between the MLP and the Church, however, their numbers are increasing.

As the church bells mark the important hours of the day, so the principal divisions of the year are set out by the annual national and parochial religious feasts and processions. Besides being major religious occasions, they are eagerly looked forward to as recreational events. Though secular spectacles, such as political rallies, the government-run Carnival procession and, above all, the cinema, are becoming increasingly important, the principal amusements of the Maltese still generally have some connection with their religious ceremonies. The French Consul in Malta at the beginning of the last century described this enjoyment of religion with great eloquence:

Le Maltais a de la religion au fond de l'âme; cette religion, dont il remplit les devoirs sans ostentation, il l'aime autant plus qu'elle prend sa source, non seulement dans une foi sincère, mais encore dans cette habitude, contractée dès l'enfance, de chercher au sein des cérémonies religieuses un délassement, que les autres peuples trouvent dans les spectacles et les réjouissances publiques.[1]

People from all parishes come to take part in the diocesan celebrations of St. Joseph the Worker, Corpus Christi and Christ the King. These rallies and processions are usually held in Valletta and Floriana. The national festival of St. Paul's Shipwreck in February, which is also the titular feast of a Valletta parish, draws many people into the city. Another national feast commemorates the lifting of the great Turkish siege in 1565. This feast coincides with that of the Nativity of the Virgin Mary on September 8, and is celebrated with boat races and other aquatic competitions in the Grand Harbour. But the traditional national festivals for the country people are the feasts of St. Gregory in April and SS. Peter and Paul (L-Imnarja) in June. Though most of the pageantry of the former has been abolished, the custom of going for a picnic to Marsaxlokk, the little village just beyond the terminal point of the procession in Żejtun, lingers on. On the occasion of the feast of SS. Peter and Paul, thousands proceed to the Buskett, Malta's only wood, where they spend most of the night before the feast eating, drinking and singing. On the feast day they throng to see the agricultural show in the Buskett, the religious procession in Mdina and the bareback horse races that take place just outside Rabat. While these two feasts are the occasions for special outings for the villagers, they are generally looked upon as very low affairs by many from the professional and middle classes.

The principal religious spectacles, however, are those which are organized at the village level. During the course of a year in Kortin, for example, there are fourteen major celebrations and

[1] M. Miège, *Histoire de Malte* (3 vols., Paris, Paulin, 1840), III, 168.

religious processions. The greatest concentration of ceremonies is around Easter. This cycle starts with the feast of Our Lady of Sorrows on the Friday before Palm Sunday. Virtually all the inhabitants escort the statue through the principal streets of the village. This is followed by the Palm Sunday procession around the church square.[1] On Maundy Thursday there is a long service during which the parish priest washes the feet of twelve village laymen. Immediately after this the church is draped completely in black damask, and a huge wooden rattle replaces the church bells as a sign of mourning. On Maundy Thursday and on Good Friday in the morning, family groups visit the church and, passing before the statues depicting scenes from the Passion, stop to pray before the elaborate Sepulchre constructed in one of the chapels. Members of each of the village associations and clubs visit the Sepulchre in groups. Many families make pilgrimages to the churches in the twelve other parishes which hold Good Friday processions. At each one they offer prayers before the Sepulchre and pause to examine the statues and funereal hangings of their rivals before going on. All morning visitors from outside stream into Kortin to see the church. Then, at about two in the afternoon, there is a three-hour sermon on the Passion. This is followed by the Good Friday procession.

Old Manwel, the procurator, directs the procession. This is his big day. During the preceding weeks, he and Anton and Pawlu, the two men who take charge of decorating the parish for special occasions, worked very hard getting ready the eight statues, assembling the ornate Sepulchre and collecting the £90 required to meet the expenses of the Holy Week. Since he became procurator twenty years ago, Manwel has collected almost £3,000 for new statues, costumes, banners and black damask for the church. The procession itself lasts about three hours. Some 420 men and youths from the village carry and escort the eight huge statues. Some of the men have carried the same statue for years. The ten who carry the statue of the Crucifixion have protected their right to do so by a notarized contract with the parish priest. In return they have spent almost £200 over the past ten years to

[1] Instead of palm fronds, olive branches are distributed to the faithful. It is generally believed that if these blessed branches are burned, their smoke is particularly effective against the harmful effects of the evil eye. Farmers pass burning leaves through their cattle sheds, and I have met professionals who do the same to their salons before cocktail parties.

repair and improve the statue and its pedestal. The procession also includes a dozen or so masked penitents who walk barefooted or crawl the length of the procession route dragging heavy chains behind them. It is a most solemn and impressive spectacle.

Very early on Easter morning the bells ring out the announcement of the Resurrection, and the sacristan, helped by Anton and Pawlu, removes the black damask from the church walls and sacred pictures. Later in the morning the procession with the statue of the Risen Christ passes through the village.

II

Of all the village feasts, the most important is always that of the patron saint of the parish church. The patron or titular saint of a church is the saint under whose special protection its founders have placed it. The titular of the parish church thus becomes the patron saint and protector of the village. In addition to the more usual religious ceremonies and processions, the people express their devotion to their patron with band marches and tremendous displays of fireworks. These celebrations provide the chief public entertainment of the countryside.

But the annual festa is more than a superior religious feast and a time of amusement for the village; it is also an event upon which village prestige depends. During the feast thousands of people crowd in from every part of the island. All these visitors have definite ideas on how a good festa should be run, and nothing they see or hear escapes their critical attention. The decoration of the church, the lighting of the streets, the quantity and firing rhythm of the exploding rockets are compared with those of their own and other feasts. The reputation of the village depends upon their judgement. This is a matter which concerns everyone, and the village draws together to display itself to the outsiders in the most favourable light. House fronts are repainted and new clothes are bought or made. The church is illuminated, the interior is hung with red damask and its treasures are placed on display. Every year the village tries to acquire at least one new work of art for this display. The principal streets and the square are lined with vividly painted papier mâché statues of prophets and saints, interspersed with urns from which sprout dazzling branches of electric light. Overhead, scores of colourful arches, strung from house to house, transform the streets into gaily lighted tunnels. The pjazza is usually draped in flags, and all the clubs are also dressed in their festal finery and their doors thrown open to the public. Many bands are hired and the mountains of fireworks are fused and made ready. All this is done before the visitors from outside arrive, and involves a great deal of organization, time and money.

The festa is thus an occasion on which communal values are re-affirmed and strengthened, as individuals and groups express their loyalty to their patron saint and unite to defend and enhance the reputation of their village. At the same time, the central position which the Church occupies in the social structure is strongly reinforced, for the parish church is the hub around which this festive occasion turns.

A festa is also an occasion on which the bonds of kinship are reinforced, for each family opens its doors to its relations, especially to those who live in other villages. Grown sons and daughters return to their parental home, forming, for a few hours, a grand family with a depth of three or four generations. Because of this influx of relatives, younger children learn to recognize more distant relatives whom they might not see at any other time of the year, and become aware of the network of kin relations that stretches out from their home. As parents become momentarily more indulgent during the festa and relax their watchfulness, it is also a favourite meeting time for courting couples and a traditional occasion on which marriageable boys and girls are introduced to one another.

The celebration of a village festa usually lasts three days. It consists of religious ceremonies, which take place principally within the church, and secular celebrations outside the church. The Maltese themselves make a distinction between these two elements in the festa: they call the former the 'internal feast' (il-festa ta' ġewwa) and the latter the 'external feast' (il-festa ta' barra). These often take place simultaneously. The mixture of sacred and profane which results was shown to me very vividly during one of the first festas I attended. I was in the church during a particularly solemn moment in the service of worship. Suddenly there was a nerve-shattering burst of fireworks from the roof of the church. Then, slowly, the sharp smell of burning gunpowder began to drift in through the open doors and mingle with the pungent odour of candles and incense. After that I ceased to be

aware of their separateness, and realized that both incense and
gunpowder were ingredients basic to the celebration of a festa.

The actual celebration of the feast can be divided into three
parts: the Triduum or Novena – the three to nine days of spiritual preparation which precede the feast day – the eve of the feast,
and the day of the feast. As the feast is usually celebrated on a
Sunday so that more people can come, the Triduum days are
Wednesday, Thursday and Friday. High Mass is offered on these
days, and in the evenings outside priests often come to preach
sermons on religious topics related to the life of the patron saint.
They are also days of preparation during which the elaborate
street decorations are hoisted into place. Throughout the day the
village is psychologically conditioned to the festa by salvoes of
aerial bombs which are often timed to coincide with the ringing
of the Paternoster and the Angelus. On the last day of the Triduum, after the final sermon, the village band marches through
the main streets. Often the band is preceded by a mass of dancing
and shouting enthusiasts of both sexes, who wave coloured
scarves, silver loving cups and other symbols of their loyalty to
their band and their saint. In villages where there are competing
band clubs, this demonstration often provokes fights between
rival supporters. These skirmishes are usually sparked off by the
bands of girls who hoarsely shout themselves into a frenzy pro-
claiming the virtues of their saint and the shortcomings of their
rivals. There are no visitors during this part of the feast.

On Saturday, the eve of the feast, there is a High Mass and Te
Deum to mark the end of the Triduum. This is usually followed
by a barrage of aerial fireworks. The local band then often
marches through the village, stopping at all the clubs for drinks.
This march is usually quite gay but in some villages it degenerates
into a drunken spree. During the day, outside priests are brought
in specially for the festa to hear confessions in the church. In the
late afternoon, visitors begin to arrive to watch the Translation, a
ceremony during which the celebrant, usually the Bishop, takes a
relic of the saint on a short procession outside the church. After
the Translation, the various guest bands march through the
village and then settle down to play selections from operas and
works composed by Maltese bandmasters. The many relatives and
friends of the bandsmen join the gaily dressed crowds who have
been streaming in by bus and car or on foot.

For several hours they wander up and down the principal streets, past the nougat vendors, past the dazzling houses with their doors and shutters thrown open to attract the eyes of all to festal drapes and carpets, gleaming cookers and new refrigerators. The crowd moves on past the packed bars and through the festooned clubs, their silver trophies all on show. Stopping now and then to eat and drink and talk with friends, they move into the church and past the banks of flowers that stand before the statue of the patron saint. From there, now surrounded by the red damask and the cut-glass crowns suspended from the golden ceilings, they pass before the silver altar-front and gaze at the jewel-encrusted reliquaries on display beside it. Now and then there is a soft discussion of price and craftsmanship as a new picture or silver candlestick reaches past the guttering candles for the attention of the crowd. Slowly, for many stop to kneel and say a prayer, the people move out through the door and past the bandstand, and on to make the round again.

The climax of the evening comes at eleven o'clock, when the forest of standing fireworks which have been planted in the square is lighted, and the second day of the festa closes in a shower of sparks and acrid smoke.

On the morning of the feast-day, there is a Solemn High Mass during which some noted clerical orator delivers a lengthy and bombastic panegyric of the saint. After the service the committees of the various clubs make formal calls on each other and exchange hospitality. The parish priest and the village clergy also call on each of the clubs and associations. Following this, the people retire to their houses for huge luncheons with their close relatives. In the late afternoon the long procession with the statue of the saint slowly moves from the church. The saint, carried by white-robed members of the confraternities, stops on the threshold to take the salute of 21 petards and barrage of smaller rockets, the *kaxxa nfernali*, which often last up to twenty minutes.[1] As the saint at last leaves the church he is cheered on his way by groups of shouting devotees. The crowds are thicker than the night before, and amuse themselves in much the same way. There are also more bands, and sometimes as many as five will be

---

[1] These petards are usually immense. They are often made from half-gallon tins packed with gelignite that is either stolen or extracted from dud shells and bombs fished up from military target areas by festa enthusiasts. Occasionally their explosions break windows.

competing for the attention of the crowd within a few yards of each other.

All the while, the procession, followed by a few black-clad penitents, solemnly passes through the main streets of the village. Often those carrying the saint move with a shuffling step that causes him to bob and turn as though he were dancing. As he passes under balconies his cheering and clapping admirers shower him with confetti. Then, as the procession nears the church, the final *kaxxa nfernali*, this time of coloured rockets, is touched off. In some villages the saint is turned around so that he can see this barrage and the display of multi-staged rockets that follows it. The statue then enters the church and the Benediction is given. After this the crowd of visitors quickly disperses. Soon the inhabitants have the village to themselves again. As the women and girls wheel and pull the children off to bed, the men carry around from club to club the grimy, soot-stained men who made and fired the fireworks. They are the heroes of the hour. Other men seek out their clubs or usual cafés and toast one another and the success of their feast. So ends the festa for another year.

The organization of the annual festa requires a long period of planning and preparation. This work calls for a certain degree of centralization. In most villages the parish priest controls the organization of both the internal and the external feasts. In some villages, however, he delegates some of this work to a procurator, usually a priest, but occasionally to a committee of leading personalities of the village. In other villages, all the details of the external feast, including the fund raising, are handled by the band club committees. In any case, the parish priest always has the last word. Sometimes there is friction between him and other interested parties over organizational details.

The cost of these feasts varies considerably. It is naturally related to the size of the village and to the degree of enthusiasm with which the festa is celebrated. It ranges from a few shillings per family in a large urban parish to as much as £15 per family in a small rural parish celebrating a particularly important festa. The average cost to the community, however, is about £1,000. The organizers of the festa collect the necessary funds by means of lotteries, fairs, special appeals and a small weekly contribution of threepence or sixpence from each family. Most fund raisers also solicit pledges from leading citizens and enter their names and the sums pledged on a long list. This method, called *l-arbural*, permits donors to compare their contributions with those of others. Then there may be several unofficial groups who raise funds for fireworks, which they manufacture and fire as their special contributions to the feast.

While I was living in Farruġ, the village celebrated the centenary of St. Martin, the titular saint of the parish. The festa cost a total of £1,465, Of this sum the parish priest raised and spent £302 for the elaborate internal feast, of which he took complete charge. The rest, some £1,163, was collected and spent on the external feast by the committee of the St. Martin Band Club. The fireworks, including most of the gunpowder, were made illegally by the members of the club in their houses and in sheds and abandoned quarries surrounding the village. The cost of the raw materials amounted to £712. Committee members divided the actual work among themselves, and set up sub-committees dealing with decoration, music, fireworks and fund-raising. With the exception of the extra lighting for the streets and the church, which was done by an outside contractor, all the work involved in the festa was done by local inhabitants.

In Kortin, on the other hand, the parish priest personally controls every aspect of the festa. With the assistance of the Sodality of Our Lady, he collects all the funds. Most of the street decoration is done by Anton and Pawlu, who get a number of people to help them. In the following table, I have summarized the rather complicated accounts of the 1961 festa in Kortin.

TABLE 3. Kortin 1961 Festa Accounts

INCOME	£	s.	EXPENSES	£	s.
Internal Feast			*Internal Feast*		
Collections	143	10	Music	150	0
Special gifts	121	10	Other	50	0
External Feast			*External Feast*		
Three collections	221	10	Decorations, programmes,		
Weekly 3d.	120	0	etc.	39	14
Lotteries	90	0	Fireworks: crackers and		
'Arbural'	53	0	ground display only	105	16
			Bands: 8 performances	224	10
			Lighting	170	0
			Balance	9	10
Total	£749	10	Total	£749	10

In addition to the sums which the parish priest spent on fireworks, another £472 was collected by six groups of enthusiasts
and spent on raw materials for the fireworks which they manu-
factured. The total cost to the village was thus £1,212. In all
respects this was an average festa for a village of 5,000.

The festa in Kortin has not always been controlled by the parish
priest. Dun Bert, the present incumbent, had something of a
struggle to seize and hold the reins of authority. Until he took
over the parish eight years ago the external festa had been run by
a committee. Though the parish priest was *ex officio* head of this
committee, the actual affairs of the committee were run by old
Manwel and the father of the curate, who was general manager of
the festa for over thirty years. The committee also included the
latter's wife's father and brother in its membership. His brother
was killed twenty-five years ago in an explosion which wrecked
the village's officially licensed firework factory and killed four
others. This committee used to book the bands, repaint, erect and
store the decorations and collect all the funds for the external feast.
One of its major responsibilities was to run the two large fund-
raising fairs which were held every year in the school. Next to the
festa, these fairs were the favourite amusement of the village. Thus
when Dun Bert arrived in Kortin, he found his was only a nominal
role as far as the external festa was concerned. As he is a man who
likes to run things his own way, the arrangement did not suit him.
Moreover, he was concerned with the financial position of the
parish, and in particular with the interest on the £3,000 that his
predecessor had borrowed from the Curia to help finance the
unfinished parish hall. To be able to meet all the parish's financial
commitments, he felt that he had to have control of all its financial
resources. The first year, however, he did very little about it.

During his second year in Kortin, the newly elected Labour
Government came to his assistance, albeit unwittingly. The new
Minister of Education refused permission to the organizers of the
Kortin festa to hold a public fair in the school. This deprived the
organizers of their major source of income, and threatened the
festa. Dun Bert quickly took over the financial management of
the festa and made two house-to-house collections. These raised
the necessary funds and saved the festa. He then gave to the
Sodality of Our Lady the responsibility of collecting threepence
a week from each household. But for six months of the year these

contributions would be used for the general needs of the church. The festa committee was dismissed.

The following year he ran the festa himself. It was quite a success, although there was some grumbling that there was not the same spirit in the festa as before. But following the festa the year after that, the grumblers became more vocal and began to take action. Their main criticism was that without the committee to whip up enthusiasm for the festa, the village was becoming apathetic about its celebration. Moreover, with no committee there was no one to paint and care for the festa furnishings – which they considered to be the finest in Malta, if not the world – and they would soon be spoiled. Consequently, a few days after the festa, the ringleaders gathered in the football club and formed a committee with Sur Ġorġ, the president of the Social Club, as chairman. Sur Ġorġ,[1] a wealthy middle-aged bachelor, is the last descendant in the village of a family which has played a leading role in the community for almost a century. The committee was composed of members of the band club, the social club and the football club. Representatives then went to Dun Bert and told him that many people wished to have the old festa committee restored, with the power of raising funds. They also suggested that this committee should control the collection of threepence a week. Dun Bert replied that while he was not opposed in principle to the idea of such a committee, he would have to consider it. In any event, he could not approve of their financial proposals. When the spokesman told him that a committee was already in existence and working for the good of the village, he became somewhat alarmed. The following Sunday he defended his position before the village from the altar, citing relevant portions of Canon Law and describing the parish's financial situation.

Sur Ġorġ's group then distributed leaflets to each house asking for a vote of confidence. This divided the village into two factions, for there were many who would not consider going against the wishes of their spiritual shepherd, no matter what their views on the festa were. Dun Bert eventually agreed to the formation of a parish council, to comprise two representatives from

[1] The title *sur* (from *sinjur*, sir, gentleman) is a mark of respect bestowed by villagers upon all educated outsiders who have no other title. It also marks social distance. Very few persons are addressed this way by their fellow villagers. Sur Ġorġ, though born in Kortin, was addressed this way because of his high social status and university education.

each association, including the religious ones.[1] The committee forwarded the names of the representatives of its three constituent clubs to Dun Bert. After some time, when they had received no reply from him, they wrote to the Archbishop. Finally, some two months later, Dun Bert wrote back that he could not accept any member of a political party committee on the parish council. This was clearly aimed at the secretary of the band club, who was a very active member of the Labour Party committee, the only political committee in the village. He was not willing to step down, and the other members of the committee supported his decision. The rest of the village slowly lost interest in the matter. The parish priest thus had his way, and is still in full control of the feast.

Many are still bitter about the manner in which their request to take a more active part in the organization of their feast was suppressed, but most have accepted it. They miss not so much the old festa committee, the members of which most people criticized freely, as the feeling they had had of all working together for the greater glory of the village. The members of the old committee at least had the virtue of being from the village, and were as anxious as the next person to celebrate the biggest and best feast in Malta, or so I was often told. Although no one suggested that the parish priest is anything but scrupulously honest, they consider that as an outsider, he does not have the same keen interest in their feast, and in the reputation of the village. Others, less charitable, accuse him of being hungry for power and anxious to enrich himself with his fees as procurator of the festa. Many also spoke to me with regret of the passing of the annual fairs, which the parish priest has not attempted to run on his own. The fairs were exciting occasions on which young and old, rich and poor, competed against each other in games of chance and raffles to win back the rabbits and chickens which they had previously donated to the festa. They say they miss the sense of unity that the fairs brought them. 'In those days we knew each other better,' one priest remarked. 'With the fair some of the poetry of the village was destroyed.' Perhaps, without expressing it in quite this fashion, the organizers of the committee, in their own way, were also seeking this lost poetry.

---

[1] Such parish councils have from time to time been established in some of the larger villages and towns, but most of them came to threaten the authority of the parish priests, who therefore disbanded them.

III

A previous chapter set out the hierarchical organization of the Church. It was observed that rank was determined by seniority in combination with certain marks of honour conferred by ecclesiastical authorities in recognition of merit. Besides rank, these honours often bestow the right to certain external signs, which are much prized. The many religious processions and ceremonies provide occasions on which parishes can display their symbols of rank to outsiders. For example, the Canons of a Collegiate church wear distinctive ceremonial robes, and are permitted to carry a huge silver mace in processions as a sign of their church's rank. They add a great deal of colour and pageantry to the religious processions in which they are invited to participate. An old man once described Collegiate churches to me as 'the ornament of all other parish churches', and added, 'where there are no Canons, there is nothing in a procession.' The clergy of a church which has received the title of Basilica may carry in procession a huge red and gold damask umbrella. They are also permitted to carry a bell, to wear gold buckles on their shoes and, on certain occasions, to say Mass facing the congregation. As with the title Collegiate, the title Basilica can only be bestowed upon a church by Papal sanction. In Malta it has been given only to the Collegiate churches of Senglea and Birkirkara, to the churches of Mt. Carmel and St. Dominic in Valletta, and in Gozo to that of St. George in Rabat.

The bestowal of honours is not in fact determined by merit alone. In view of their importance as symbols of excellence, they become counters in the competition between parishes and between parish associations. Their acquisition is thus a matter of great concern to the entire community, and often becomes the subject of political action. That is, persons and groups try to influence those who make the decisions in relation to their bestowal. Through their network of personal relations, leading village figures, including the priests, try to influence the Bishop and the monsignori who surround him. They also bargain with these authorities, and if an unfavourable decision is handed down, they may resort to an open show of disrespect towards the Bishop – by smashing his coat of arms, for example – to signal their dissatisfaction and so attempt to force him to reconsider their

claim. The final decision is thus made in response to a great many
pressures. The honour usually goes to the contender who can
present the best case and apply the strongest pressure. This is
normally the largest and most influential of the groups competing
for the honour. Thus the number and degree of honours bestowed
on any group are roughly equal to its social importance to the
community of which it forms part.

The current dispute in Gozo over the bestowal of the title of
Basilica on the church of St. George provides an excellent illus-
tration of the length to which the pursuit of such honours may be
carried. For many years the Collegiate Chapters of Nadur and
Xaghra unsuccessfully sought to obtain this title for their respective churches. During that time the Bishop had been able to avoid
having to commit himself. In Nadur many believed that their
church would be the next in Gozo to become a Basilica as a compensation for certain privileges which were modified some thirty
years ago. The people of Xaghra, for their part, were also under
the impression that their church would become the first Basilica
in Gozo.

The claims of Nadur and Xaghra were not the only ones. There
was also that of the new parish which the Bishop had created
around the church of St. George in Rabat. Many argued that this
new parish should take the lowest position in the diocesan table
of precedence. But the new parish was located in the island's
capital, and many of Gozo's most influential citizens had been
instrumental in bringing about its creation. Moreover, the church
of St. George was one of the oldest in the diocese. In brief, the
thought of their parish having an inferior rank to that of the small
rural parish of Munxar, hitherto the lowest-ranking parish, was
distasteful to the townsmen. As a Basilica the church of St. George
could take precedence over all other parishes and occupy a place
immediately before the Collegiate Chapters. The partisans of St.
George were in an excellent position to make their voices heard
in the Curia, and late in 1958 the title was formally bestowed upon
their church. The people of Nadur and Xaghra, led by their disappointed Canons, reacted with great vigour. The abuse and
violent action that resulted were as insulting to the Bishop as
anything that the Labour Party has been accused of directing at
him or at the Archbishop of Malta.

Nadur and Xaghra all but severed relations with the Curia.

Both boycotted the annual festa of St. George, and in 1961 some hot-heads in Xagħra even erected a road block to prevent cars from the village going to Rabat. The people of Nadur refused to celebrate their own festa, or to take part in the St. Gregory procession. They also refused to allow the Bishop to administer the sacrament of Confirmation in their parish. In Xagħra someone exploded a bomb on the roof of the Archpriest's house because many considered that he, an outsider, had not worked hard enough to secure the Basilica. In 1960 Xagħra celebrated only the internal festa, and even that was not without incident. Shortly before the festa, the Bishop received an anonymous letter accusing him of being an enemy of the village. Later, when he visited the village to assist at the High Mass, he was given a hostile reception. Then it was discovered that part of the throne that he was to sit on during the service was missing. Furious at these insults, he issued formal interdicts against the person or persons unknown who had written the anonymous letter and 'stolen' his throne.

To date the dispute has not been settled. The people of Nadur and Xagħra both say that peace cannot be restored until they receive some other honour to compensate them for the lost Basilica. To back up their claims, they have each spent tens of thousands of pounds during the past few years decorating their respective churches. In Nadur the new marble pulpit cost almost £5,000, and the work of covering the walls with marble may cost as much as £20,000 before it is completed.

This type of dispute, however, is not limited to Malta's sister island. The Collegiate Chapters of Birkirkara, Senglea and St. Paul's Shipwreck in Valletta have similar unresolved conflicts over precedence, and they refuse to take part in processions together. But not all their disputes are limited to matters of precedence. In 1949 the people of Birkirkara smashed the Archbishop's coat of arms and heaped rubble in the main door of their church, thereby symbolically denying him entrance. They were protesting because the Archbishop had abolished, among others, the right of the Chapter to choose as Canons only those priests born and baptized in Birkirkara. The Holy See was able to resolve the dispute, and a few years later it bestowed the title of Basilica on the town's church.

IV

Even when a parish is not competing with another for some honour, the decoration of the parish church is a matter of great concern to the village. As we have already observed, a parish church is more than just a central place of worship; it is the centre of most of the social life of a village and the repository of its collective wealth. The building itself, with its gilded ceilings and silver altar fronts, its damask tapestries and embroidered vestments, its precious votive offerings and ornate statues, represents a fortune amassed over centuries from the savings and bequests of countless inhabitants. The parish church is thus the embodiment of village history, a showpiece which all, even the most anti-clerical Labour supporters, point out with great pride to strangers.

The custodian of the church is the parish priest, who is responsible for all alterations or improvements to it. He often delegates much of this work, especially the fund-raising, to a local priest, who then becomes procurator of the church. Many church procurators devote their lives to building and beautifying their churches, and every generation contributes thousands of pounds for its upkeep and embellishment. But regardless of who holds the procura of the church, the people regard it as their communal property, and all take an intense interest in its maintenance and decoration. Because of this proprietary interest, a difference of opinion over details of decoration, and especially over structural alterations to it, can divide a village into strongly opposed factions.

At the beginning of this century Kortin was divided on the question whether to enlarge the existing church or to build a new one. The stronger faction, which included the resident nobles and the wealthy merchants, wished to build a new church. Their leader was Sur Vinċenz, the grandfather of Sur Ġorġ. A wealthy merchant was thought to be willing to help finance the scheme. This group was opposed by most of the village clergy, including the parish priest, on the ground that the cost of a new church was beyond the resources of the village. Moreover, a benefactor had already bequeathed £2,000 for enlarging the church. The leader of this faction was Dun Batist, the senior local priest in the village.

The dispute raged from about 1880, when the plans of the new church were drawn up, to about 1913. In 1898 a number of people addressed a petition to the Archbishop requesting permission to build a new church. But a year and a half later he ruled in favour of a counter-petition, and gave permission to begin reconstructing the old church. Shortly after this a riot developed out of a meeting called to urge the parish priest to permit the building of a new church. During the commotion, the stone railing around the front of the church was damaged. Six days afterward forty-two people were arrested for disturbing the peace and taken off to prison. After three days the arrested men were released because of insufficient evidence. The court assessed the total damage to the church railing at twenty-two shillings. This incident aroused the village. A month later the new church faction decided to begin work without the permission of the Archbishop. Early the following Sunday, a huge crowd led by Sur Vinċenz asked the parish priest for permission to work on Sunday. When their request was refused, they set off for the site and began to work anyway. That afternoon, Sur Vinċenz hired a band to play for them, and the music attracted people from many surrounding villages. The following day Dun Batist and the parish priest laid the matter before the Archbishop.

All through the month of October 1901 the leaders of the new church faction went in delegations to argue their case before the Archbishop, who was on holiday in Marsalforn, Gozo. The local diarist, on whose account much of the above is based, notes cynically that the Bishop listened with great attention, as he was in debt to one of the leading members. Meanwhile, the parish priest had been able to mediate between the factions. Dun Batist and his followers agreed to stop their work on the old church provided their opponents reimbursed them for their expenses to date. This was arranged. Finally, in January 1902 the parish priest announced that the Archbishop had given his permission for the construction of the new church. That afternoon there was a great celebration in the village, with many fireworks and a guest band, again paid for by Sur Gorg's grandfather.

But the construction of the new church soon ran into trouble. Sur Vinċenz failed to raise the capital required. As Dun Batist had foreseen, the cost of this grandiose scheme was far more than the village could manage. After the foundations had been laid, the work gradually came to a halt. The village did not begin to re-build the old church until the end of 1909, when the parish priest set out to raise the extra £2,000 required. One of the fund-raisers at the time was young Manwel, the father of Dr. Farrugia, who had then just begun to teach in the village school. The reconstruction of the old church was finally completed in 1913.

Sur Vincenz gradually dropped out of village activities. Many people blamed him for the trouble in the community. In 1912 he refused to allow the organizers of the festa to anchor one of the major street decorations in its customary position against his house. This action created more hostility towards him, and shortly after the festa a bomb was thrown through his cellar window. During the next six weeks he and his close relatives received several threatening letters, and one night the front of his house was smeared with red paint. But the rivalry between the factions gradually died out, and today there is no trace of it left. The old men of Kortin who now spend their days in the shade of the huge façade of the church, and their evenings on its cool steps, remember the struggle clearly, for they were all deeply involved in it. As they look back to the events of sixty years ago, they often remark with wry smiles that the village was then a very lively place.

This incident was exceptional because of the immense cost to the village in money and labour that the construction of the new church involved. Now that church-building is no longer in vogue, new works usually take the form of decorations, such as new paintings or candlesticks. These do not generally arouse strong feelings, since all additions to the beauty and wealth of the church are normally welcome. A wise priest, however, tries to ensure that there is general agreement about them. It sometimes happens that he forgets, or underestimates, the proprietary interest of his parishioners in their church. When this occurs, there is usually trouble.

Some years ago, the parish priest of Farruġ proposed to regild the chancel. His parishioners welcomed the idea, and contributed generously. But when the work was finally completed and the scaffolding removed, his parishioners were shocked to find that he had placed his personal coat of arms high over the chancel. He was the first priest in the history of the parish to have put his coat of arms inside their church; moreover, he had done so without their consent. There was great indignation, but the arms remained there. A year later he was promoted to a larger parish, and left the village. People then began to ask the new parish priest to have the coat of arms removed. He quite understandably declined to do so.

One morning, less than two months after the old priest had left, the village was startled by the news that the irksome coat of arms had been removed in the dead of night by persons unknown. In its place gleamed the freshly painted arms of the village. The job, which had involved at least three men, one of whom must have worked on top of a 60-foot ladder, had been skilfully executed. To add insult to injury, the nocturnal painters had telephoned the former parish priest after finishing their work and announced that he would find something of great interest in the church next time he visited Farruġ. The following morning he came to the village, saw what had happened to his coat of arms, and immediately reported the matter to the police. The police interviewed many people, but did not find the culprits. They are still looking for them. The village is quite pleased that the arms were removed, although some deplored the rather crude way in which it had been done.

CHAPTER VI
Festa Partiti

Village unity is an ideal, and all villages try to present a tightly united front to the outside world. In spite of this, all are divided internally by cleavages which cut across the community at various levels. Some of these divisions are only temporary, and disappear when the issues out of which they have arisen are resolved. Others, which may have arisen out of temporary issues, have for one reason or another become a permanent part of the social scene. But regardless of their origin or duration, these divisions are painfully real to the villagers. Persons made vulnerable through a network of personal relations are often forced to commit themselves to a particular division. In doing so, they become opposed to neighbours and kinsmen who are committed to the other side. This is one of the characteristics of life in all small villages. It is particularly true of communities, such as those in Malta, in which the inhabitants are closely related through kinship and affinity.

The Maltese call these divisions *partiti* (sing., *partit*). The term thus corresponds not only to groups of the order which we in English would call 'parties', but also to those to which we would apply the term 'factions'. Political parties are called partiti, and so are rival groups such as the two in Kortin which competed over the rebuilding of the church. Partiti are said to have *pika* between them. *Pika* denotes relations of competition, ill-feeling, hostility. There is little about the word which suggests the good-natured competition that can exist between rival school football or cricket teams. On the contrary, if there is *pika* between two groups, a no-holds-barred competition is expected. Partiti are thus considered to be a bad thing. They disrupt the harmony of the community and make it more difficult to project the ideal image of village unity to the outside world.

The oldest permanent division that exists in the villages is between the supporters of rival band clubs. This division is related to the cult of saints. In the previous chapter it was noted that besides the patron saint, parishes celebrate many other saints. The feasts of these secondary saints are normally not as lavish as the annual festa of the patron. But many villages celebrate two large festas: one for the titular saint of the parish, and the other for a secondary saint who has assumed almost equal social importance. Where this occurs, a village is divided into two partiti, each of which has its own band club and celebrates one of the saints. The partiti compete over almost every aspect of the festa, including the decoration of the streets, the adornment of the statue, the number of guest bands and, above all, the fireworks. Even the exact number of communicants, the size of candles and the quantity of light bulbs illuminating the façade of the church often become the subject of dispute. Farruġ is divided by this type of rivalry. One partit is dedicated to St. Martin, the titular of the parish, the other to St. Roque.

The origins of these festa partiti, where they can be traced, are very much alike. Most of them came into existence sometime between 1850 and the turn of the century, and most arose out of disputes between persons concerned with the celebration of the titular festa and those interested in the cult of some lesser saint. The latter were usually members of the confraternity dedicated to that saint.[1] These factions in time became centred on separate social clubs, and eventually acquired brass bands. The clubs provided a permanent institutional basis for the rivalry. As time went on, the partiti became more violent in their disputes and in the pressure they put upon individuals to support them. Finally in 1935, the Church, long alarmed at the extremes to which the devotion to some saints had been carried in certain villages, took steps to eliminate the competition. It promulgated a series of regulations designed to reduce the scale on which secondary feasts could be celebrated. These stipulated that for secondary feasts there was to be no Translation of Holy Relics on the eve of the feast, that only the church and the area immediately adjacent to it could

---

[1] Cf. Rob. Miṛsud Bonnici, Ġrajja Tal-Mużika F'Malta u Għawdex (Malta, Giov. Muscat, 1954), pp. 38 f. He suggests that these partiti developed out of a dispute between persons who wanted to play sacred music by the Maltese composer Vinċenzo Bugeja (1806–60) and those who preferred that of his rival, Paolo Nani (1814–1904). As far as I could determine, however, the only partiti which arose directly out of this dispute are those in Żebbuġ. On the other hand, many rival partiti, once established, played the music of either Bugeja or Nani during their feasts. The former took a star as their symbol, the latter an eagle. Today partiti in many villages are still nicknamed either tal-istilla or tal-ajkla after this once-important division.

be illuminated and that only one band on the eve and one on the day of the feast would be allowed. Although they are now ignored, the regulations also placed limits upon the variety, quantity and duration of firework displays. Finally, they drew attention to the already existing regulations that church decorations and new works of art introduced for secondary feasts should be less costly and beautiful than those for titular feasts.[1]

Parish priests were expected to insist on the observance of these regulations, and they succeeded so well that some secondary feasts were reduced to minor celebrations. Moreover, the *pika* between the partiti in Żabbar and Qrendi was so violent that the secondary feasts there were suppressed completely.[2] This served as a stern warning to others.

II

The story of the origin and development of the festa partiti in Farruġ is in many respects similar to the accounts which I collected about festa partiti in other villages. It might, therefore, be helpful to examine it in some detail. Before 1877 there were no festa partiti in the village; everyone co-operated in the celebration of the feast of St. Martin, the patron of the parish. By all accounts it was a humble one, and lasted only one day. This period is described as an idyllic time during which the village was happy and united. But in 1876 a new parish priest arrived, and after that the scene began to change. Dun Rokku, the new priest, not only had a strong personal devotion to the saint after whom he had been named, but he was also from a village where there was a strong secondary partit devoted to St. Roque. Within a year he established a confraternity dedicated to St. Roque in order to 'inject some more life into this rural parish', according to the president of the St. Roque Band Club. The first feast in honour of St. Roque was celebrated in October 1878 to mark the establishment of the confraternity. Although the new secondary feast was at first a simple affair, it and the titular feast grew during the next

---

[1] Concilium Regionale Melitense (1935), *Decreta* (Malta, Empire Press, 1936), p. 91.

[2] In Żabbar the devotion to St. Michael, the secondary patron, died out almost completely, though the *pika* between the bands has persisted. But in Qrendi the devotion to Our Lady of Lourdes, the secondary patron, has continued as strong as ever. In 1958 the Archbishop reinstated the confraternity dedicated to her, which his predecessor suppressed in 1935, but the partit band is still not allowed to play for her feast.

few years. In 1880 the new confraternity dedicated an altar in the
church to its patron, and by 1886 some persons were beginning
to grumble about having to pay for another feast. There was a
feeling of 'you collect for your feast, and we'll collect for ours.'

In 1888 an incident occurred which changed the course of the
rivalry between the supporters of the two saints, which until then
appears to have been rather mild. Dun Rokku, who was the procurator of the parish church, tried to increase the rent on some of
the local property it owned. There was an outcry, and some persons went to the Bishop to complain that not only had Dun
Rokku been diverting parish funds to buy new street decorations
for the feast of St. Roque, but he was also raising rents to continue this work. The complaints resulted in an investigation, following which the procura of the church was taken from Dun
Rokku and given to a prominent member of the village, who
favoured St. Martin. This action, not surprisingly, infuriated Dun
Rokku. From that day onward, so the accounts relate, he threw
his full support openly behind the feast of St. Roque.

Some time after this, the partiti each formed their own social
clubs. According to St. Martin supporters, their club grew out of
a pre-existing band club, but that of their rivals was not established until after the First World War. They thus consider that
they have seniority. St. Roque partisans, on the other hand, deny
this seniority. They maintain that both clubs came into being out
of the former club around the turn of the century. Consequently
they have equal seniority. However, both clubs claim that the
records crucial to the question of seniority were destroyed by
enemy action during the last war. There is thus no documentary
evidence for either claim, a fact which makes for deadlock when-
ever the issue of seniority is raised.

Dun Rokku was a strongminded priest, and he ruled the village
for fifty-six years. When he finally died in 1932 at the age of 90, he
was blind and deaf. During his many years in the parish he did
much to beautify the church. Unfortunately, so people recount, he
also introduced the hated partiti that divided the village. Through
a variety of means at the disposal of a parish priest, he succeeded in
wooing or coercing three-fourths of the village into his partit.
There are many stories about the old man and the methods he
used to recruit supporters. One is that he would make it difficult
for people to marry unless they were, or became, members of the

Confraternity of St. Roque. Unfortunately, at this point, it is not possible to distinguish fact from myth. The tales are accepted as reality, and so help to formulate the attitude of St. Martin supporters toward their rivals. However, when the old priest died, it was discovered that most of the festal finery of the parish church had been purchased in the name of the Confraternity of St. Roque. St. Martin supporters were in the humiliating position of having to beg their rivals for the use of the church valuables in order to decorate the church for the feast of the parish patron. Moreover, while the old priest had controlled the celebration of St. Martin, he had allowed the lay leaders of the St. Roque partit a free hand in planning their feast.

At this time the St. Martin club was split over national politics, and a faction composed of Strickland supporters left and founded a new club. Though both clubs remained loyal to St. Martin, there was trouble between them. Older St. Roque partisans recount with amusement how a report to the police by the secretary of the parent club resulted in twenty members of the new club being arrested and fined for gambling. But the hostility between these two factions declined when Strickland made his peace with the Church, and in 1934 they reunited.

The burden of redressing the balance between the partiti fell upon the old priest's successor, and upon those who followed him. There were many incidents between these priests and the St. Roque partit, and on several occasions the former had to send for police protection. In spite of the 1935 regulations, the St. Roque partit retained its numerical superiority as well as the church decorations during the 'thirties. It was not until 1942 that a shrewd parish priest succeeded in bringing the silver altar front out of the St. Roque strongroom into that of the parish church, where it has remained ever since.

The rivalry between the partiti lay dormant during the Second World War, as the people united to fight for survival. But it flared up again immediately after the war, as did similar rivalry in other villages. Both clubs organized musical bands for the first time. After a series of incidents which culminated in the parish priest again having to send for police protection, this time against angry St. Martin supporters, the rivalry began to decline somewhat. This decline was brought about chiefly by the effects of emigration, improvements in local transport, the establishment of a number of new associations in the village and the increased activity of political parties.

During the mid-'fifties emigration drained away many of the most active supporters of the partiti. In 1954 alone, no fewer than two dozen men between 18 and 38 left the village for Australia and Canada. Each club lost key bandsmen, and the two bands, already heavily bolstered with outside players, never recovered. A constantly improving bus service enabled young men to go to the 'talkies' in other villages, or just stroll up and down Kingsway in Valletta – a very popular pastime with young people from all over Malta – instead of spending the evening in their village clubs. During this period the Football Club, MUSEUM and Catholic Action were established in the village and began to draw potential partit leaders into other spheres of activity. The Football Club was particularly damaging in this respect. As a neutral social club it provided a place where the young men of the two partiti, who normally never entered one another's clubs, could meet. A number of friendships developed between them, and it soon became the most popular club in the village. Finally, the increased activity of the national political parties during the elections in 1950, 1951, 1953 and 1955 drew the attention of the villagers away from purely parochial concerns and bound them up in rivalries of a different order, which often cut across traditional allegiances. This created factions within the clubs and weakened the partiti.

Rivalry flared up again in 1960, when the supporters of St. Martin, intent upon celebrating the centenary of their patron, staged the greatest festa in the history of the village. But the political and religious fervour of the 1961 election campaign soon captured the attention of the partisans, and the festa of the following year was a pale shadow of the gala spectacle of the year before.

Before proceeding any further, we must unravel the rather complicated tangle of partit, club and confraternity. All festa partiti are composed of three groups: (i) the band club, which provides the leadership of the partit and includes most of the active male supporters, many of whom are also members of (ii) the confraternity allied with the partit or dedicated to its patron, and (iii) the rank and file of men, women and children who are members neither of the confraternity nor of the club, but still support the partit against its rival. The central strand running through all these groups is the loyalty of the people to the partit and its patron, shown by supporting the many activities that the leaders organize, and by boycotting similar activities of their rivals. These include fund-raising lotteries and fairs, weekly collections and partit picnics and pilgrimages. During the festa, supporters march with the statue, dress themselves and their houses up and in general celebrate their patron. Their rivals often walk about unshaven and glowering, and do not normally decorate their houses.

Although most people in a village divided by this type of rivalry will choose, or be forced, to take sides, a few are able to avoid this commitment, or at least say they have. These are often priests and teachers, who sometimes find it to their advantage to remain neutral, as do outsiders who have married into the village. MUSEUM members are not permitted to maintain partit affiliation though, of course, many do. Neutral people contribute to both feasts. A true partisan would never contribute to the external feast of his rival, although he might give something to the parish priest for the internal feast. During periods of intense rivalry, even these contributions cease. Thus, virtually the entire £1,465 which St. Martin's centenary cost was contributed by his supporters alone. Six months later their rivals spent £600 on the feast of St. Roque.

The band club is the organizational and social centre of a partit. All members of the club are supporters of the partit, but not all supporters of the partit are members of the club, though nonmembers are normally welcome to come and use its facilities. To a certain extent, membership of the club depends upon the availability of ready cash, for many men are reluctant to part with the subscription fee as long as they can make use of the club's premises. Though the confraternities are open to all adults without regard to partit affiliation, there is normally a positive correlation between partit and confraternity membership. Generally speaking, the supporters of the titular feast enrol in the older confraternities of the Blessed Sacrament and the Holy Rosary. These confraternities are established in all parishes, and play an important part in many religious ceremonies. Supporters of the secondary patron enrol in the confraternity dedicated to him, if they feel inclined to join one.

These general principles can be illustrated by data collected in Farruġ. Table No. 4 below shows the relative strengths of the two

5. Fireworks for the feast of St Leonard

6. 'Viva San Ġużepp!'

partiti. Of the 617 inhabitants of both sexes over twenty-one years old, 48 per cent support St. Martin, 42 per cent St. Roque, and 10 per cent are uncommitted. Although the numerical strength of the partiti is almost the same, each claims two-thirds of the total population. Of those who claim to be neutral, 63 per cent were born outside the village.

TABLE 4. Farruġ: Festa Partit Affiliation and Place of Birth

PARTIT	PLACE OF BIRTH			
	Village	Outside	Total	Percentage
St. Martin	250	47	297	48
St. Roque	219	42	261	42
Uncommitted	22	37	59	10
Total	491	126	617	100

Table 5 shows the relation between partit affiliation and membership in one of the three confraternities in Farruġ. Of the members of the Blessed Sacrament and the Holy Rosary who belong to no other confraternity 84 and 64 per cent respectively belong to the St. Martin partit. Ninety-five per cent of the members of the Confraternity of St. Roque belong to his partit. It is interesting to observe that 83 per cent of those who declare that they are not committed to either partit have also avoided confraternity membership.

TABLE 5. Farruġ: Festa Partit Affiliation and Confraternity Membership

CONFRATERNITY	PARTIT			
	St. Martin	St. Roque	None	Total
B/Sacrament	57	8	3	68
St. Roque	5	87	–	92
Holy Rosary	20	8	5	33
Mixed	24	23	2	49
None	191	135	49	375
Total	297	261	59	617

Recruitment to a partit is quite straightforward, for members do not now change sides, although this occasionally occurred in the generation following their establishment. Today a person is either born into a partit, or marries into it. Children support the partit of their parents, and an outsider marrying into the village generally supports that of his (or her) spouse. Marriages between members of rival partiti are regarded as undesirable. They occasionally take place, but the division of loyalty within the nuclear family which results often leads to quarrels and, occasionally, to temporary separations. (The favourite festa-time story of the wife who refuses to cook for her husband because he belongs to the other partit is based on fact!) Of the marriages contracted within Farruġ, 72 per cent took place between members of the same partit. Children of mixed marriages support the feast of their favourite parent: boys normally follow their fathers and girls their mothers.

I recorded only two cases in Farruġ of adults who changed their partit affiliation. Both occurred over fifty years ago. A leading member of the St. Roque partit left it after a heated quarrel with Dun Rokku over the design for new street decorations. He subsequently became one of the other partit's most honoured members, and even wrote a book on the life of St. Martin. The second man left St. Roque when he married the daughter of the president of the St. Martin club. I was told that the girl's father had insisted on the change before he gave his consent to the marriage. The young man went on to become president of the club, as did his only son. In another village a few young men left their partit after a quarrel with one of the leaders, but all returned after a year.

Although an outsider who marries into a village generally supports the partit of his spouse, a few of them, particularly the men, succeed in remaining neutral. Of the 122 outsiders who married into Farruġ,[1] 28 per cent of the men but only 8 per cent of the women remained uncommitted. A few even chose to support partiti opposed to those of their spouses. Thus a women from Qrendi who married a St. Martin supporter and moved to Farruġ became a follower of St. Roque because she had been a keen member of the secondary partit in her native village. Children of families in which one of the parents is an outsider, especially if the parent remains neutral, often support the partit of their friends rather than those of their parents or siblings. A case in point is that of the president of the St. Roque club, and his brother. Their father was an outsider who, because of his position as headmaster, made a point of remaining strictly neutral. Though his wife was from a St. Martin family, one son supported St. Martin, the other St. Roque.

[1] 61 men and 61 women. These marriages represent 54 per cent of the total in the village.

Children begin to express partit affiliation when they are between twelve and fourteen years old. At this age they are old
enough to follow the processions and take part in the demonstrations on their own. Fund raisers make demands on them, and they
are asked to help decorate the streets. At this age they also begin
to play in the band. A youngster would jeopardize his social
standing with his elders and with his age mates if he failed to take
a firm position with regard to one of the saints. This would
remove him from much of the community's social life. Consequently, by the time a village boy has reached fifteen, he has
usually selected his partit, thus accepting and becoming part of the
fabric of partit rivalry which will hold him until he dies or leaves
the village.

There is some relation between occupational class and partit
affiliation: in general, the supporters of titular saints belong to a
higher occupational class than their rivals. The reason for this will
be discussed a little later. The data I gathered in Farruġ illustrate
this correlation clearly. As shown in Table No. 6 below, 83 per
cent of the village's professional and white-collar workers belong
to the St. Martin partit, while only 38 per cent of those engaged
in agriculture do so.

TABLE 6. Farruġ: Partit Affiliation and Occupational Class

OCCUPATION		PARTIT AFFILIATION		
		Percentage of		
	Number	*Lab. Force*	*St. Martin*	*St. Roque*
Professional and clerical	12	4	83%	17%
Service and skilled	115	39	55	45
Semi- and unskilled	124	42	48	52
Agricultural	45	15	38	62
Total	296	100		

So much for the origin and social composition of the partiti. I
may just observe here that festa partiti are not usually based on
territorial divisions. Since upward mobility does not involve
change of partit, but is often accompanied by a change of residence, all residential areas are mixed. Nonetheless, there is a tendency for supporters of the titular partiti to live in the better
residential area near the church, and for their rivals to live in the
poorer sections more remote from the central square. This is a
reflection of the differing occupational class of the members. This

residence pattern is certainly true in Farruġ, and I observed much
the same thing in other villages divided by festa partiti. In Farruġ,
65 per cent of the people living on the main square and the four
streets leading into it supported St. Martin, but only 46 per cent
of those living in other parts of the village did so.

Disputes between partiti usually concern matters of precedence
or their ability to display devotion to their saints. Each partit has
certain rights, usually secured at the cost of clashes with its rival.
These include the position and participation of the club and confraternity in Church processions and at other functions, the routes
over which these processions travel and the possession of certain
property and its display in the parish church. Any attempt to
extend or reduce them is resisted by the partit affected, which
takes action to protect its interests by trying to influence the
Church authorities, who must make the final decisions.

The structural position of a partit determines the kind of
pressure that it can bring to bear upon the Church. Those of
titular saints are, in a sense, the establishment parties. As we have
seen, the Church seeks to build up their celebrations at the
expense of the secondary ones. Hence a titular partit can negotiate
from a strong position: its ultimate sanction is refusal to participate
in the feast of the village patron, an event which the Church is
anxious to see celebrated with great pomp. Secondary partiti, on
the other hand, are inherently opposed to the Church in matters
of festa policy. They try to increase the scale of their feasts, while
the Church tries to reduce them. They dare not cancel their feasts
for fear that the Church would accuse them of making trouble
and suppress them, as it did the secondary festas of Our Lady of
Lourdes in Qrendi, and St. Michael in Żabbar.

Their position in opposition to Church policy has given most
secondary partiti a certain *esprit de corps* and unity of purpose that
their rivals often lack. This has made them better able to with-
stand the divisive effects of the political factions which have
recently weakened many of their rivals. It has also generally
resulted in the emergence of stronger leaders. Secondary partiti
are often united around a single professional class leader who can
not only hold the partit together in the face of the attacks of its
opponents, but can also argue intricate points of Canon Law with
the monsignori at the Curia and, at times, with the Archbishop
himself. As we have observed, the secondary partiti generally have

fewer professional class members. Consequently competition for the role of leader does not occur so often, and there is a longer tenure of office. In the partit of a titular saint, with its better-educated members, there are more men with the necessary qualities of leadership, and accordingly more competition for office and a high turnover of office holders. The competition both creates and results from internal factions which weaken the group. In Farruġ, for example, the President of the St. Roque Band Club has led the St. Roque partit more or less continuously since Dun Rokku died thirty years ago. He is also just about the only member of the partit with the educational qualifications and social position required of a leader. The key positions of the St. Martin Band Club, in contrast, constantly pass between about half a dozen educated persons. This divided leadership has weakened the club; and on one occasion it even split in two. The strong leadership and internal unity of the secondary partiti, plus the fact that they rarely present claims that are not well founded, has enabled them to score many successes in spite of their apparently unfavourable position in relation to the Church.

Disputes between festa partiti are all very much alike. A typical dispute begins when leaders of a secondary partit petition the parish priest for some new privilege, for example the right to renew the bouquets of artificial flowers which adorn the statue of their saint. The parish priest normally refuses at first, and tells them that he thinks the old flowers are quite serviceable. His policy is to let sleeping dogs lie. Moreover, he has to take into account the rule that decorations for secondary feasts must not be more beautiful than those for titular ones. But the saint's supporters continue to bring influence to bear on him. In the meantime, members of the titular partit have learned of their rivals' move and rush to the parish priest to point out that the old flowers are more than adequate. They threaten to cancel their feast if he gives in on this matter. The priest is now caught in a vice, and the pressure on him builds up. Finally, he agrees to refer the whole case to the Curia and passes the matter upwards, usually with a feeling of relief. Relations between him and the partiti return to normal, as the scene of the struggle shifts to the Curia.

The Curia normally appoints experts to re-investigate the merits of the case, including the proposed design of the flowers. Leaders from both partiti spend a great deal of their time at the

Curia trying to persuade all concerned, from the Bishop down, to think the way they do. This may go on for years, for the Curia, knowing the trouble that lies ahead, is usually in no hurry to give its decision. When the final decision is handed down, it is usually favourable, and the design for a set of flowers less beautiful and costly than the corresponding set of the titular partit is furnished. The secondary partit then instructs the craftsmen to begin work. The titular partit announces to everyone that it will cancel its next feast.

It often happens, however, that just before the new bouquets (or whatever *objets d'art* are concerned) are inaugurated during the secondary festa, the parish priest discovers that most of the Curia's specifications have been ignored. The new flowers are far more beautiful than they were supposed to be. He is furious. The guilty leaders of the secondary partit apologize profusely and take immediate steps to make them less beautiful. Occasionally, the priest may discipline the partit by temporarily reducing the scale of its feast. The secondary partit then holds its feast, and the flowers are admired by all visitors. Strong police reinforcements usually prevent trouble from occurring. Relations between the parish priest and the titular partit are gradually re-established and it agrees, usually for some concessions on his part, to celebrate its feast again. But in a year or so, a new dispute occurs, and the process starts all over again.

Sometimes relations between a parish priest and a partit reach a deadlock that can be broken only by an outside peacemaker, frequently an officer of the police. The police in any case have a vital interest in the degree of rivalry existing in the villages, as it is their business to keep order during the feast. The number of police on duty at these times ranges from a dozen or so in villages such as Siġġiewi and Naxxar, where there are no partiti, to around 100 in those where there are strong ones, such as Mqabba and Żurrieq. Occasionally a parish priest is threatened, frightened by a home-made bomb, or attacked; he then often requests, and generally receives, a transfer to another parish.

So far only the more important encounters between partiti have been discussed. There are many other events to keep their rivalry alive throughout the year. The numerous fund-raising fairs of the band clubs are occasions for the village to divide along festa partit lines. While supporters of the partit running the fair flock to it, their rivals invariably stage their own fair or, and this is more usual, hire several buses and noisily leave the village for a picnic or a pilgrimage to some shrine of their saint. Many other incidents divide groups and associations along partit lines. For example, a former head teacher of the Farruġ school told me that he had once tried to get the girls to wear the dark blue hair ribbons which are supposed to be part of their school uniforms. He was astounded when half the girls flatly refused. It was then explained to him that blue is the colour of the St. Roque partit, so the St. Martin girls could not be expected to wear it.

Let us now look at some of the major skirmishes which have taken place in Farruġ during the last ten years. During 1952 and 1953 there was a dispute over an attempt by the St. Roque procession to pass along a street over which St. Martin's followers claimed exclusive rights. When the inexperienced new parish priest backed the St. Roque claim before the Archbishop, he brought violently into the open a dispute over which his predecessor had successfully procrastinated for years. The followers of St. Martin not only refused to celebrate their feast, but also succeeded in frightening the unfortunate priest rather badly by exploding a huge rocket in the drainpipe under his house. Some St. Martin partisans gleefully recounted to me that the priest was soon transferred to another parish, and that during his last week in Farruġ he had asked the police to escort him between his house and the church. Relations between the Church and the St. Martin partit were restored when the Archbishop modified the St. Roque procession route.

In 1956 the St. Martin Band Club refused to celebrate the titular festa because the Archbishop had given the Confraternity of St. Roque permission to renew the four bunches of artificial flowers which decorate the main altar during his feast. The following year the St. Roque Band Club refused to play at the installation ceremony of the new parish priest because the Curia had just turned down the confraternity's request for permission to hang a new picture over its altar. In 1960 the same priest angered the St. Roque partit by refusing to let it participate in the St. Martin centenary celebrations. The poor man's hands were tied, for the St. Martin club had declared that it would have nothing to do with the feast if its rival took any part in it. At the moment, there is another struggle in the offing. The Confraternity of St. Roque recently petitioned the Archbishop for permission to renew the platform on which their saint stands during the feast. St. Martin supporters have threatened to cancel their feast if permission is granted, as it probably will be, for the present platform is old and falling to pieces.

While I was in the village, there was also a dispute over precedence between the two band clubs on the occasion of the installation ceremony of Dun Franġisk, the present parish priest. This is a good example of a dispute over precedence, and it is one which recurs in some form every time a new parish priest is appointed to a village where there are two band clubs. The band which has precedence has the right to march last and to escort the priest from the church to his house after the ceremony. The other club escorts him from his house to the church before the ceremony. Quite straightforward, but clubs rarely agree on which one has precedence. The dispute thus presents a knotty problem that brings a new priest abruptly up against the realities of parish politics within a few days after his arrival. His handling of the matter may well govern his relations with the partiti during the rest of his time in the village.

On the evening when Dun Franġisk moved into the parish, the St. Martin Band Club gave a party to welcome him and to bid farewell to his predecessor, who had been its strong ally. The party was a great success. The departing priest received a huge coloured portrait of St. Martin as a farewell gift, and Dun Franġisk met all the St. Martin leaders and blessed the club's new television set. A few days later, the St. Martin leaders called on the new priest and offered to provide a musical escort to and from the church for his installation ceremony. This was to be followed by a concert in the square and a firework display. The offer pleased him and he accepted. During the next few days the St. Martin club went about collecting the £25 the band programme would cost, thus advising the village of its plans.

Until then Dun Franġisk had heard nothing from the St. Roque club, a fact which rather disturbed him.

Two days later he called in person at both clubs to invite them to attend his installation ceremony and the reception following it. But he found the clubs deserted. The members of the St. Martin committee were away offering their congratulations to the old parish priest, who that night was holding his installation ceremony in his new parish. Most of the St. Roque leaders, for their part, were off supervising a fund-raising fair which they had hastily organized to help ensure that no St. Roque supporter would be tempted to attend the lavish reception of their former antagonist. Finding no one of importance at the clubs, Dun Frangisk left the invitations with the bar-keepers.

Two days later a group of St. Roque leaders called to thank him for his invitation, at the same time informing him that they were looking forward to escorting him to and from the church with their band. Dun Frangisk had been warned by his predecessor that this might happen, so he asked them to meet him the next evening to discuss the details of the programme with the other club.

Next morning the members of the St. Martin partit were furious over this move of their rivals. They grumbled to me that now only a miracle could save the band programme they had been planning. It was the main topic of conversation in the village that day. Many people were on hand to watch the St. Martin committee members enter the parish priest's house that afternoon. Soon after, the rival delegation, headed by the vice-president, the secretary and the treasurer of the St. Roque Band Club, joined the meeting. The first session lasted two hours. I saw the young priest shortly afterwards. He looked rather stunned, and exclaimed, 'They can't agree. They both want to escort me to my house! It's like a U.N. session. Nothing is settled and we meet again in an hour.' I learned later that he had had a difficult time preventing the rivals from coming to blows.

They met again, but the deadlock remained unbroken. The St. Martin delegates maintained that their club had the right to escort the priest to his house because it was the oldest, it represented the official patron saint of the village and it had been the only one to play during the past two installation ceremonies. Their rivals rejected all these claims, and suggested that they draw lots for the privilege of playing last, or hire outside bands to play, and let them decide. The St. Martin representatives rejected these suggestions. Finally, at midnight, the parish priest put an end to the wrangle. He told them that unless they could decide the matter among themselves, he would have to decline their offers to play for him. He asked them to let him have their decision by the following evening.

The next day each delegation called separately on Dun Fran-ġisk and told him that they had not been able to reach a decision. In fact, they had not met again. St. Martin supporters were very bitter about the whole affair, and said that since they could not play, they would also cancel the firework display they had been planning.

The installation ceremony took place three days later as planned. Neither band played, but each fired off a number of petards during the day, and each gave the newly installed priest a rousing salute of fire crackers on his return from the church. The leaders of both partiti attended his reception, separately to be sure, and they were very cordial in their congratulations. The skirmish was over. St. Martin leaders admitted to me that Dun Franġisk had handled himself well, and that he had taken the only sensible course open to him. They declared, however, that he should not have called in person to invite the St. Roque club, but should have sent the more usual printed invitation. The St. Roque leaders, on the other hand, were quite pleased with the way things had gone. They invited Dun Franġisk to a reception in his honour at their club the following week, and shortly after-wards asked him to support their request for a new platform for their saint.

This whole episode must be seen as an attempt by the St. Roque partit to unseat its rival from the position of pre-eminence it had enjoyed during the centenary celebration. It could do this by blocking the St. Martin club's plan to be the only band to play at the installation ceremony. The St. Roque leaders were able to make their first move when Dun Franġisk called in person at their club, thereby assuring them that they be given equal standing with the other, which they felt had been favoured by his predecessor. They would not have made their offer to play if there had been the slightest indication that Dun Franġisk was going to favour their rivals. In fact it is extremely unlikely that the St. Roque club was really planning to play. It had not done so for many years, it had no bandsmen and at the time it did not even have a band-master. Finally, it had made no collection to pay for a band. All these facts were known to the St. Martin supporters when they made their offer to play. Furthermore, they had heard indirectly from the St. Roque secretary – who told a policemen in a neigh-bouring town, who in turn mentioned it to the president of the

St. Martin club – that the St. Roque club was not planning to participate in the ceremony in protest against the way they had been
treated during the centenary. Dun Franġisk's spontaneous move
upset their plans.

Although Dun Franġisk favoured the suggestions that the clubs
draw lots, or hire outside bands, St. Martin rejected both because
they implied that the clubs had equal status. The last time the St.
Roque band had played was six years and four parish priests
before, when the local police inspector had devised a compromise
solution, and the St. Martin leaders had 'allowed' St. Roque to
play the last march of the day, while their band escorted the new
priest home. They believed any concession they made now would
undo the advantage which they felt they had gained as the only
functioning band in the village during the past six years.

Thus it came about that no band played at Dun Franġisk's
installation ceremony. This greatly surprised the many visitors
from the city and the suburbs, but the good people of the district
found it quite in accordance with the way things should be, considering the issues involved. At no point in the series of events
were the feelings of the young priest, whom all liked, ever considered. His installation had become the vehicle for a clash between the followers of St. Martin and St. Roque. They had been
vying with each other for supremacy long before he was born,
and would be at it long after he left. Any concessions made for his
sake would have to be entered into the eighty-year-old ledger of
credits and debits, and might have an important bearing on the
outcome of the next series of encounters.

III

Two interesting problems remain to be considered: why festa
partiti arose during the fifty years or so after 1850, and what
reasons prompted people to join one partit rather than its rival.
The factors which caused the partiti to come into existence at this
particular period in Maltese history are necessarily complex, and
they are dimmed by the time that has elapsed since their foundation. Nonetheless, one can discern several elements which would
appear to be related to the general problem. To begin with, during
this period there was a sudden increase in the devotion to the
Virgin Mary following her apparition in 1858 at Lourdes, and the

definition of the dogma of her immaculate conception four years earlier, and to St. Joseph, who was declared patron of the Catholic Church in 1870. Virtually all the secondary partiti are dedicated to one of these two.[1] At the same time, there was a general elaboration of the celebrations connected with the cult of saints, including the Italian and Sicilian custom of having bands play during the festas.[2] These were but a part of the more general influx of Italian ideas and customs which accompanied the refugees from Italy of the Risorgimento, who streamed into Malta following 1850. The propaganda efforts of the pro-Italian politicians of the time assisted in the diffusion of these customs, especially in the urban areas.

During this period a conception of social organization new to Malta was also gaining currency, namely the idea of voluntary associations for laymen, and in particular, social clubs for 'gentlemen'. After the establishment in Valletta of the exclusive British Union Club in 1826 and the equally exclusive Casino Maltese in 1850, clubs of various kinds began to spring up in many villages. They multiplied so rapidly that a local chronicler wrote in 1890, 'Today you don't find a village without one or two, nor a city without three or five.'[3]

The latter half of the last century was a period of relative economic prosperity for Malta. This resulted from the increase in military and naval activity after the outbreak of the Crimean War; the sharp expansion in government spending on public works programmes from 1859 to 1865; and the renewed world demand for Maltese cotton as a result of the cotton shortage created by the American Civil War.[4] The economic boom increased the demand for unskilled labour from the villages. This, in turn, helped to disseminate urban-Italian cultural traits. It also provided a financial basis which permitted increased expenditure on festa decorations, fireworks, and above all, uniforms and instruments for the bands. Finally, this period saw the establishment of government schools in all the villages. City-born schoolmasters moved into rural

[1] See Appendix A.
[2] See, for example, Giuseppe Pitrè, *Feste Patronali in Sicilia*, vol. XXI of *Biblioteca delle Tradizioni Populari Siciliane* (Torino-Palermo, Carlo Clausen, 1900), *passim*.
He also indicates that a number of Sicilian towns and villages are divided by rivalry between supporters of different saints. (pp. xlvii ff.)
[3] P. P. Castagna, *Lis-Storia Ta Malta* (3 vols.; Valletta, C. Busuttil, 1890), III, 128.
[4] Charles A. Price, *Malta and the Maltese: A Study in Nineteenth Century Migration* (Melbourne, Georgian House, 1954), pp. 105 ff.

communities where they became leaders, and the source of many new ideas and customs. In Għaxaq, for example, I found that a teacher born in Valletta had been the one to introduce the custom of decorating the streets for the festa.

It is, of course, extremely difficult, if not impossible, to discover the motives which prompted people to choose a particular partit. The only possible clue to at least one set of reasons may well lie in the correlation between occupational class and partit affiliation. Apart from this class alignment, I found no evidence in Farruġ, or any other village so divided, of any pre-existing structural division out of which these festa partiti might have developed. In view of the way membership is inherited, it would appear that the position which members of the great-grandfather generation occupied in the village class structure in some way influenced their choice of partit. There is some evidence for this, although not a great deal, to be found in the genealogies of the present generation. Frequent marriages with outsiders, emigration and the changing employment structure of the country over the past six decades have blurred this picture considerably.

But it is certainly possible that the new cult appealed more to those persons who held no office in the older confraternities and who performed no official functions in connection with the celebration of the annual festa of the village patron. Through the new cult they could gain offices and perform functions which hitherto had been monopolized by the circle of the village elite who surrounded the parish priest. Some informants have also mentioned that young men were particularly attracted to the new cult. In this we can see the universal resistance of the young to the authority of their elders, for by becoming active in the new cult, they were asserting their independence from the controls of the older generation. Were the secondary partiti then a form of protest against the established authority, a sort of underdogs' party?

Other facts appear to support the hypothesis that the foundation of the secondary partiti was in some way related to a wider working-class movement. Many of the partiti are dedicated to St. Joseph, the patron saint of the working classes who were beginning to organize themselves into formal associations throughout Europe. In Malta there are many signs that this devotion was very strong. In addition to the many new confraternities dedicated to him after 1850 (in Naxxar, Għargħur, Kirkop and Xagħra, for example) he was chosen as patron of the new parish churches of Kalkara, Qala and Msida. Moreover, four parishes have secondary feasts dedicated to him (Rabat, Għaxaq, Kirkop and Żebbuġ). Besides these Għargħur and Siġġiewi had St. Joseph partiti which succumbed to the 1935 Church regulations.

The identification of secondary partiti in general with St. Joseph is also perhaps reflected in the colour most have chosen as their symbol. It is blue, the colour of the banner of the Confraternity of St. Joseph. The supporters of many secondary partiti, even if their saint is the Virgin Mary, wave blue scarves about to show their loyalty to it. Their rivals display red scarves, after the colour of the banner of the Confraternity of the Blessed Sacrament, whose members support the titular saint.

The correlation between partiti and occupational class is also shown in the high proportion of village priests who are sons of families supporting the titular feasts. I once asked the leader of a secondary partit why this was so. He replied that it was only natural since the families of the titular partiti were in much closer contact with the parish priest. Thus their sons, rather than those of rivals, more often became his young helpers and altar boys and received the necessary recommendations to the seminary and other church-run schools. From there, some became priests, and others assumed positions of leadership with the various associations. Other informants suggested it was because the 'best' families support the titular saints, and therefore can afford the additional school fees and loss of earning power that are involved in having their sons become priests.

Of the 41 priests born and now resident in Żurrieq, Kirkop, Qrendi, Mqabba, Luqa, Għaxaq and Żebbuġ, 33 (80 per cent) are sons of families supporting the titular feasts. This percentage gains added importance by the fact that in each of these villages the secondary partit is either equal to or larger than the titular partit. The exception is Żebbuġ, where the secondary partit is decidedly smaller than the titular one. In Farruġ, though the local priest is from a St. Roque family, all the offices connected with the parish church, and 23 of the 30 key positions with Catholic Action, the Football Club and the Labour Committee, are in the hands of St. Martin supporters. Thus the members of titular partiti are not only closer to established authority, they often become part of it.

Whatever the reasons for their beginnings in particular villages, there are today festa partiti or at least competing band clubs in nineteen villages and towns. Ten communities are divided by the type of rivalry described above. Of these Gudja has partiti which compete only over two secondary feasts and another, Żebbuġ, has three rival band clubs, two of which compete over the titular feast. Besides these ten, another four towns are divided by rivalry between their constituent parishes, five more are divided by rival band clubs not related to the cult of saints, although the band clubs in one of them, Żabbar, were once allied to festa partiti.

The competition between rival parishes of the same town is very similar to that between festa partiti. In fact the division of Qormi and Rabat (Gozo) into two parishes each came about partly because of the rivalry between festa partiti. Since each parish has its own church and is not limited by the 1935 regulations, the competition between them is even keener than between festa partiti within the same parish. For this reason the feasts of St. Mary and St. George in Rabat (Gozo) and St. George and St. Sebastian in Qormi are probably the most spectacular in the country. Competition between rival band clubs not related to the cult of saints, in contrast, is not as fierce as that between festa partiti. It is, nonetheless, a considerable force in the communities where it exists. Disputes between these band clubs usually involve questions of precedence, such as those which arise over their positions and role during the titular festa or at an installation ceremony of a new parish priest. Failure to reach agreement may mean that one or both boycott the celebration.

Finally, weak festa partiti once existed in another seven villages. But as they were not aligned with band or social clubs, they were not well enough organized to resist the firm pressure the Church began to exert after 1935. Today there is scarcely a trace of their former existence. All festa partiti and rival band clubs, both present and past, are listed in Appendix A.

IV

Implicit throughout this examination of the various types of competing groups described in this chapter and in the previous one, has been the highly formal nature of their interaction. Their disputes are like war games. The action between them takes place within a framework bounded by the decrees of the Church, the laws of the State and the appropriate body of custom. New pictures are not hung in churches and new procession routes are not followed unless permission has first been obtained from the Church. Action without this permission could result in the suppression of the feast, the desecration of the church or the interdiction of the ringleaders. In the same way, the threats and insults of demonstrating partisans rarely result in physical violence because of the swift penalties that the ever-vigilant police would impose. Permanent truce or peace between the partiti and competing parishes is impossible to achieve owing to the inherent nature of the rivalry which exists between them. It is this state of continuous one-upmanship that provides the driving force behind much of the village politics in Malta. At least it did until the increasing involvement of the people in national politics created a new set of conflicting loyalties that cut deeply across many older ones.

7. Demonstrations of loyalty to the Archbishop

8. Labour Party supporters cheer Dom Mintoff

CHAPTER VII

National Politics and the Village

In the last few years issues of national policy have taken an increasingly important place in the villages alongside the purely parochial ones we discussed in the preceding two chapters. Divisions based on opposed political ideologies are now reflected in the groups and associations in which people spend their time. The major division which cuts across all Maltese villages is based not so much upon rivalry between political parties, as upon the present conflict between the Malta Labour Party and the Church. But as has been observed, conflict between the Church and a political party is not new to Malta. It also existed during the late 'twenties and early 'thirties.

The dispute between the Labour Party and the Church is essentially a struggle for power. Dom Mintoff, the Labour leader, accuses the Archbishop Gonzi of siding with Britain to maintain Malta's colonial status, and with interfering in politics by attacking the Labour Party and its leaders. In its 1962 Electoral Manifesto the MLP proclaims the right of a person 'to fulfil his civic duty without pseudo-religious interference'; sees as a crime 'any interference with the right of a democratically elected majority to implement the people's mandate', and advocates the 'abolition of medieval privileges which have retarded [the country's] social and economic progress.'[1] The Church sees this not only as a direct attack on the basic right and duty of a bishop to teach and to guard the morals of his flock,[2] but also as a move to destroy its traditional position in Maltese society. In particular it fears that if the Labour Party were returned to power, it would enact legislation which would render the Archbishop liable to prosecution before the criminal court if he were to comment on the political issues of the day.

These opposing views are expressed in the slogans written on

---

[1] See Appendix B for the 1962 MLP Electoral Manifesto.
[2] Cf. William E. Addis and others, 'Bishop', A Catholic Dictionary, pp. 80 ff.

walls and shouted at public meetings. Mintoff is portrayed as a Socialist devil working to give the islands over to Communism in the manner of Cuba's Castro. These are some typical examples of the ones that appeared on the blackboard outside the Kortin Catholic Action centre: 'Mintoff is the enemy of the Church', 'Nobody can serve both God and the Devil', ' "The Bishops are interfering in politics!" That is what Communists say,' and 'We don't want Communists among us!' In stating their case, Mintoff and his supporters did not mince words either, as the following slogans that appeared on the blackboard of the Kortin Labour Party club demonstrate: 'We want a chance in court about the $60,000 lie',[1] 'With the Papal flag in their hands and shouting for vengeance', 'A fish begins to stink from its head',[2] and 'In Gozo they told the women that we have tails.'

The popular slogan 'Either with the Bishop or against the Church!' sums up the uncompromising attitude of the Church. Most of the sanctions it has imposed have presented that choice to the people in unequivocal terms. Early in May 1961, shortly after the Labour leaders were interdicted, all Church lay societies were instructed to obtain from each member a pledge of his full and unqualified support for the Archbishop. Those that declined to give this were expelled from the society concerned and their names reported to the national office of Catholic Action. But a more drastic sanction was imposed a few weeks later. After the Executive of the Labour Party had invited the Archbishop and the Bishop of Gozo to debate their policy in public at a Labour rally in Cospicua, the Bishops replied to this insult by issuing a circular which declared it a mortal sin to print, write for, sell, buy, distribute or read the Labour Party newspapers. All confessors were instructed to put the necessary questions to their penitents.

Hence, to remain a Labour supporter, a person has to forego the Church sacraments that he has been brought up to believe vital to his happiness and spiritual salvation. This is a very serious choice for a practising Catholic, and before these sanctions were imposed, the Maltese were among the most devoutly Catholic people in the world. It has also meant that MLP supporters cannot

[1] This refers to the Archbishop's charge, made at a rally in March 1961, that Mintoff had received $61,000 from the allegedly Communist dominated Afro-Asian Peoples' Solidarity Organization, which the MLP had just joined.
[2] A Maltese proverb meaning that corruption first becomes apparent among people in high places. This was presumably directed against the Archbishop.

act as godparents. For this reason a number of people, prevented from inviting relatives and friends to fill this office, have preferred not to baptize their children.

Many have bowed to the authority of the Church and have stopped supporting the Labour Party. But in spite of everything that has been preached on the subject, many others still feel that there is nothing incompatible between support of their political leader and loyalty to their religion. This view is expressed in the slogan which is displayed so often at MLP rallies that it has become almost a party motto: 'With Mintoff always, against the Church never.' Although they are told from the pulpit that it does them no good, most members of the Labour Party continue to attend the daily or weekly services of worship that they have been going to since childhood. Besides, many have rationalized their action by saying that the Archbishop of Malta is acting for personal and political motives; as long as the Pope himself does not condemn the MLP they will continue to support it. This attitude is reinforced by the experience of some Labour supporters who have been absolved while on holiday or on duty with the military services in countries where it is possible to be a Socialist and a practising Catholic at the same time.

As a result of these sanctions many have turned their backs on the Church and no longer attend religious services. Before this struggle between the MLP and the Church, it would have been unthinkable for anyone in a small village to stay away from church. A civil servant in one village told me that he had been a confirmed atheist for years. Yet until this past year he had gone to church every Sunday. In his words, 'People make it very difficult for someone who does not go to church, and I have to live here all my life. Besides, I might lose my job if people complained about me.' But he is now an open supporter of the Labour Party and no longer feels obliged to go to church. To some extent, then, the sanctions of the Church have created a social role for the non-practising Catholic.

The attitude of many who support the Labour Party is summed up in the words of a twenty-year-old bus conductor in Kortin. We were sitting around a table in a small wine shop when I asked him why he supported the MLP in spite of the opposition of the Church to it and the fact that Mintoff was regarded as a Communist by so many in the village. He replied in English, 'I am young, I cannot even vote in the next election. But I must think of the future. I feel that Mintoff is doing what is right for Malta. He helped the poor people when he made the government. The Church fights Mintoff because she fears she will lose her privileges and power if he wins, and that he will tax her property. The Church is in favour of keeping people ignorant, and limiting their education. Why? Because when people are educated they think for themselves and can judge. They no longer follow blindly. Besides, you should not take too seriously all this talk of Communism – they are products of this fight. In a fight, people use all means available.'

The street sweeper who was with us understood most of the conversation and shook his head in disagreement. His only comment was the proverb, 'A ship with two captains can't sail' (Il-vapur biż-żewġ kaptani ma jimxiex). At this every one in the shop nodded in agreement, for both Labour and Church supporters had different captains in mind. Those who support the Archbishop look to him as the leader of the Maltese people. They make little distinction between Church and State. Labour supporters, in contrast, make a clear distinction. Mintoff is their candidate for head of State, and since they see the Archbishop as interfering with their choice, they accuse him of reaching out to control both Church and State.

II

At the village level, this conflict has brought about a bitter division. All societies and groups which are not formally identified with one side or the other, have been divided and weakened by politically based factions. The parish priest is the leader of those who support the Archbishop. His most enthusiastic followers are the clergy and the members of the lay societies. This group, with the other prominent villagers who make up the parish priest's circle, provide the hard core of the active opposition to the MLP. Considering the offices that they occupy and the societies to which they belong, it could hardly be otherwise. They usually meet in the club houses of the societies, but sometimes the older members meet in a particular café.

The hard core of the Labour group is made up of the officers of the local MLP Committee and the members who openly frequent the club. There is very little contact between the leaders and active members of the two sides. But there are a number of persons who would like to avoid having to make a break with either side. For the most part they keep quiet about their political views. But the Church sanctions and the pressure exerted by relatives, friends and workmates is slowly reducing their numbers.

Affiliation is expressed in very much the same way as with the festa partiti. That is, supporters participate in their side's activities and boycott those of their opponents. The activities of those who support the Archbishop centre on the lay apostolate societies. The leaders of these groups, with the parish priest, usually organize the buses that take villagers to the rallies of the Diocesan Junta, which are usually held in front of the Floriana parish church. More recently, separate parishes have organized rallies and pilgrimages of reparation a few days after the Labour Party has held a meeting in the village. An official visit of the Archbishop to a village also provides an occasion for a big demonstration by his supporters in his honour. Bus-loads of colleagues from other parishes often swell the ranks of the local lay societies during their demonstrations. They in turn attend similar meetings in other parishes. Occasionally they unite and act in opposition to MLP meetings in their own and other parishes. More often though, they organize picnics or pilgrimages to take supporters out of the village when their opponents have arranged an event. Supporters of the Archbishop show their allegiance by decorating their houses with pictures of him and with yellow and white Papal flags. Many also buy the newspapers of Catholic Action and the Young Christian Workers.

Enthusiasm for the struggle, which had assumed something of the character of a Holy War when I left Malta, has gripped both young and old. For example, at an MLP meeting in Birkirkara in May 1961 I saw a black-cowled MUSEUM woman herding a group of youngsters up against a police cordon. All were blowing whistles as loudly as they could. A little later a scuffle broke out between MLP supporters and organized parties from the lay religious societies who had surrounded the meeting. But a police water cannon promptly dampened their enthusiasm. In another village, opponents of the MLP rang the bells of the parish church to drown out the Labour voices. This technique, in fact, was first used in Gozo at a big MLP rally there in April, where it proved so successful that not one of the speakers was able to make himself heard. The meeting was finally called off, and the large MLP delegation from Malta was literally routed. They had to return on foot from Rabat to the ferry, as the bus drivers refused them transport. During the long walk to the ferry, the Labour partisans were ambushed and rather badly mauled by groups of men, women and children from all over Gozo. The ardour of many Gozitans had been worked up by lay leaders who toured the villages for several days beforehand. But besides their religious fervour, there was a considerable element of parochial pride, and the feeling that 'we'll show these Maltese invaders a thing or two.' In all, forty persons were reported injured. The Gozitans were extremely proud of their victory, and the local branch of the Social Action Movement published a booklet to commemorate the occasion.[1]

The activity of Labour supporters centres on their local Party club or committee, which arranges for transportation to national MLP rallies and conducts lectures and classes on the political aims of the Party. It also organizes social evenings and outings for Labour supporters. The members of the Local Committee take charge of the preparations for national meetings held in their own village. Local Committees take the initiative in preparing floats, decorated carts and companies in costume for the annual MLP demonstration on the First of May. For the past few years the MLP Executive has also organized a carnival celebration for its supporters to induce them to boycott the official government-sponsored carnival.[2] Labour supporters read the Labour daily newspaper, Il-Ħelsien (Freedom), and the Sunday Voice of Malta. Since the condemnation, Il-Ħelsien has become a party badge. It is pasted on bus windows during MLP excursions, worn as an armband at rallies and in general used by Labour supporters to taunt their opponents. I have even seen some young men in Kortin swagger into church on Sunday morning with copies of it sticking out of their hip pockets.

All supporters of the Labour Party do not show their allegiance this openly, for many wish to avoid the break with a large section of the community which would follow such action. Some are teachers or civil servants who fear lest their open support for the

[1] Għawdex Jiddefendi L-Knisja [Gozo defends the Church] (Gozo: Social Action Movement, 1961).

[2] The government at this time was administered by a British Chief Secretary, and the MLP ordered members to stay away from all events it organized.

MLP cost them their jobs.[1] Others have friends or relatives on the other side with whom they do not wish to break. Yet others, responsible for maintaining the unity of a neutral club, fear that an open stand will bring about a crisis which would divide it. Although most of these persons continue to read the condemned papers, they do so discreetly, for reading them openly would provoke incidents. There are also a large number of Labour sympathizers who have been unwilling to forego the sacraments of the Church. They no longer read the Labour papers or attend MLP rallies, but they are bitter about having been forced to make the choice.

The physical act of purchasing a Labour newspaper has in itself become a public statement of political allegiance. After the condemnation and the threat of a general Church boycott of their premises (which was carried out in Gozo) most vendors have refused to handle MLP publications. In the villages they can usually only be bought at the local MLP club. Thus the act of striding across the village square and into the stronghold of the devil, performed in front of many of the village elders, becomes an open declaration of sympathy with the Labour cause. In Kortin many wait until the square is empty, usually around midnight in the summer, and then scuttle into the club to get their papers.

III

There is a correlation between occupational class and support for one of these two ideological divisions. In general, professionals, white-collar workers and farmers support the Archbishop, and industrial labourers the Labour Party. There are several reasons for this. To begin with, the Labour Party is a working-man's party, and there is ideological support for it on that account. Although the MLP has a definitely socialist ideology, and is a member of the Socialist International (points on which the Church attacks it regularly), it advocates few of the measures associated with doctrinaire Socialism, such as public ownership of transport and industry or the collectivization of farming. On the other hand, it does promise equal opportunity for all, and 'the right of the

[1] The Malta Government Circular of 19 October 1960 prohibited most grades of civil servants from holding office in political organizations or publicly expressing their political views. This regulation is something of a paradox in a small country in which most intellectuals work for the government in one capacity or another.

people to have the final say in the nation's vital means of production.'[1] These policies have a general appeal to labourers and
are among the reasons for the party's popularity.

The Labour Party is closer to the worker than any of the other
political parties. In this respect, its organization resembles that of
the Church. As already noted, the MLP rests on its village and
district organization. This has enabled the average worker to
have a say of sorts, not only in his party's policy, but, when it was
in power, also in the affairs of government. How he and his
neighbours were able to manipulate the party structure to their
advantage is a matter which will be discussed in greater detail in
the following chapter.

During its period in office the Labour Party did much to
improve conditions for the workers and the poor. This is another
reason why many support it. It introduced many social benefits,
including the extension of medical services, regular allotments of
free food and social assistance allowances for the needy and aged.
It also built many new schools, surfaced dusty roads and under-
took other large public works projects which gave employment
to many, besides benefiting the community. Moreover, the party
did a great deal to improve agriculture by bringing in foreign
experts who set up an advisory service and introduced new crops
and techniques of cultivation. All these and the general atmosphere of activity which permeated the Labour Government,
gained great popularity for the party and its leader.

There is yet another important way in which the MLP attracts
many: it has attacked the established authority of Britain, the
Church, the local captains of industry and the prosperous members of society. This outlook appeals not only to many poor and
underprivileged persons, but also to the young and the unin-
fluential who are seeking to establish their personal independence
and to make their mark on society. This opposition to authority
and vested interests holds an attraction for many social 'misfits',
such as the young 'Teddy Boy' element, the eccentrics and free
thinkers. These find in the MLP a haven for their nonconformity to
the social and moral teaching of the Church. Though social and
religious stigma still attaches to them, many find it easier to bear
in the company of others who have similar beliefs and problems.
The Labour Party has thus provided social outcasts with a sense of

[1] MLP manifesto. See Appendix B.

'belonging', and to a certain extent has created for them a community of their own. These persons often make up the hard core of Labour supporters in their villages, since they have nothing to lose by openly fighting the Church.

A number of sociological explanations can be advanced to account for the support professionals, white-collar workers and farmers give to the Church. First of all, professionals generally lose status in the eyes of their colleagues, if not the wider society, if they join the Labour Party or sympathize with it. It is a working-class party, and they are professionals. There are a number of notable exceptions to this, but the only professionals that I met who sympathized with the MLP were either candidates for office with it or members of the Executive. The political ideology of their colleagues and the expectations of their clients combine to make them look upon the Labour Party as the antithesis of everything they have been brought up to believe in. They, through their offices in parish associations and through their work as doctors, lawyers, high civil servants, and so on, form part of the establishment to which the Labour Party is opposed.

Much the same reasoning can be applied to the white-collar workers. As teachers, clerks and other intermediate grade civil servants they hold a relatively high position in the social hierarchy of their villages. Many are anxious to identify themselves with their social superiors, those in control of the village as well as their employers, and thus look down upon the MLP as opposed to their interests. Moreover most of them have been educated at colleges run by the Church. There their teachers gave them additional religious instruction and strengthened those values which make the anti-clerical tone of the Labour Party repugnant to them.

Farmers, on the other hand, are looked down upon by many and are regarded as underprivileged by all. Why is it then that they do not support the Labour Party? Farmers in most communities are very conservative, and those in Malta are no exception. Their solitary occupation isolates them from the Labour Party ideology which is so freely discussed among the industrial workers of Malta. Not only that, but as we have seen, they are among the most poorly educated section of the community. Many are unable to read the propaganda which the MLP disseminates through its publications. This isolation from the secular and materialistic ideologies which enter the country through the

Grand Harbour and first establish themselves in the conurbation surrounding it has helped to keep the farmer devoutly tied to the Church. For this reason the action of the MLP in challenging the authority of the Bishops is as abhorrent to him as it is difficult to understand.

The recent sanctions of the Church have increased the class alignment of those who support the Labour Party and those who oppose it. This is largely because those with high social status have more to lose than industrial workers, and are thus more vulnerable to the pressure of public opinion and the Church. The increasingly heavy pressure of the Church has forced many of the young professionals and intellectuals to abandon the party for which they voted in 1955. But even when the MLP was in office, its policies began to alarm many in the professional and middle classes. They objected not only to Mintoff's attitude to the Church, but also to the somewhat abrupt way his government occasionally dealt with the professional and business communities. Many were disturbed by the MLP's rather sudden switch from advocating integration with Britain to demanding complete independence. As most of those who left the party or became inactive in it were moderates, both in their approach to the Church and to the economic and political problems facing Malta, the MLP has become more extreme in its outlook. This in turn induced others to leave it. This process was accelerated by the regulations which prohibited the better-educated civil servants from taking an active part in the political life of their country.

Table 7 below shows the rough correlation between occupational class and support of the Malta Labour Party. In particular, it demonstrates that as the proportion of skilled workers decreases, so does the proportion of voters who support Labour. Other variables are the number of professionals and farmers. The Second and Fourth Electoral Districts polled the highest number of Labour votes in the 1962 election, and the Sixth and Tenth the lowest. The MLP polled 56 per cent of the total votes in the Second Electoral District, where 45 per cent of the working population are classified as skilled labourers.

In contrast, it received only 6 per cent of the votes in Gozo, where only 16 per cent of the people are skilled labourers, but 38 per cent are engaged in agriculture. Another important variable is the number of clergy resident in a district. The relatively high proportion of clerics and nuns in the Sixth Electoral District helps to explain the relatively low Labour poll there. It is also a significant factor in explaining the overwhelming defeat of the MLP in Gozo. These two districts have the highest proportion of clerics in the country. The Fourth District, in contrast, has the lowest.

TABLE 7. 1962 Elections:
Occupational Class and Voting Behaviour[1]

ELECTORAL DISTRICTS[2]	SELECTED OCCUPATIONAL CATEGORIES (As percentage of total lab. force)			PERCENTAGE LABOUR VOTES
	Professional[3]	Skilled	Agricultural	
IInd (Senglea, etc.)	4 (3)	45	4	56
IVth (Żurrieq, etc.)	3 (2)	34	11	47
VIth (Birkirkara, etc.)	6 (4)	33	11	24
Xth (Gozo)	7 (6)	16	38	6
All Districts	5 (3)	32	11	34

IV

It will have been observed that there is a certain superficial similarity between the reasons given here for belonging to the MLP and those suggested in the preceding chapter for recruitment into the secondary festa partiti. One might expect therefore that in comparison with titular partiti, secondary partiti would have a higher proportion of Labour supporters among their members. Unfortunately, owing to the disturbed political situation prevailing at the time, I was not able to gather satisfactory systematic data on this point. Almost all informants with whom I discussed the matter suggested that secondary partiti did in fact have more pro-Mintoff members than their rivals. But the situation is not quite as straightforward as it might appear. To begin with, the statements of informants varied according to their own political beliefs and their position in relation to the festa partiti. Rivals generally tried to place each other in an unfavourable light. Thus an anti-MLP member of a band club supporting a titular feast

[1] Source: 1957 Census: Report on Economic Activities, pp. 40–111; and The Malta Government Gazette (3 March 1962), pp. 585–94.
[2] IInd (Cospicua, Senglea, Vittoriosa, Kalkara, Żabbar, M'skala), IVth (Żurrieq, Safi, Qrendi, Mqabba, Kirkop, B'buġia, Żejtun, M'xlokk), VIth (Birkirkara, Balzan, Lija, Attard, Naxxar, Għargħur).
[3] Percentage of priests, monks and nuns in parenthesis.

would describe the rival club as a Mintoff stronghold, but suggested that his own club had relatively few MLP members. In contrast, a member of the rival club with the same political view would often say just the opposite. Parish priests generally gave very conservative estimates of the number of MLP supporters in the clubs, but usually said that the secondary clubs had more.

Another factor which makes it difficult to be dogmatic about the political alignment of the partiti is that most are located in the southern villages. These communities are reservoirs of industrial labour and are generally strongly pro-Labour. For this reason, unbiased informants generally estimated that Labour supporters made up between half and three-fourths of the membership of all clubs, but that secondary clubs had slightly more. My own experience in Farruġ confirms this. I found there that about 70 per cent of the members of each partit are pro-Labour, although the leaders of the village MLP group are almost all from the St. Martin partit. This I suggested was due more to the shallowness of the leadership resources of the St. Roque partit than to the political inclination of its members.

At the policy level, all clubs usually maintain strict political neutrality. At least, all incorporate clauses to this effect in their by-laws, and many prohibit party newspapers and political discussions in the club. Nonetheless, some clubs are closely identified with a particular political party. Of the clubs that are aligned in this way, those that celebrate the titular feasts generally support one of the parties allied with the Church, usually the Nationalist Party; their rivals support the Labour Party. This alignment often comes about when a leading member of a club seeks political office. Where this occurs, members of the opposite festa partit, as a matter of course, give their votes to his chief opponent in another party, or to a rival in his own party. The political significance of the rivalry between festa partiti will be examined in the following chapter, together with some of the ways in which political candidates manipulate the partiti, and are, in their turn, manipulated by them.

But the tendency to political polarity of rival band clubs still does not explain why the leader of a secondary club, for example, supports the Labour Party, and not one of the rival parties. The chief reason for this, quite apart from the fact that he may have a personal preference for the party, is that the members of his own festa partit form the nucleus of his political following. It is not surprising therefore that he should support the party they favour.

There is another interesting way in which festa partiti in general, and secondary partiti in particular, are related to support for the Labour Party. In all villages divided by these partiti, people have become conditioned to opposing the authority of the Church in connection with matters dealing with the celebration of feasts. This, I suggest, has enabled them to accept the anti-clerical outlook of the Labour Party more easily than the people of villages not so divided. An old stone-cutter in Kortin, who was procurator of one of the small chapels in the village, once unconsciously pointed to the structural similarity of the MLP and secondary festa partiti. We were discussing the resemblance of the Strickland crisis of thirty years ago to the present political dispute, when he pointed to the parish church and remarked, 'I've always been against them. I was for Strickland. I'm for Mintoff, and if we had partiti here, I would support the secondary feast.' There is, of course, a difference between the opposition of a secondary partit and that of the MLP. Nonetheless, both oppose the authority of the Church and both resort to attacks on the clergy to drive home their points of view. This is anti-clericalism. Both the festa partiti and the Labour Party make a distinction between the person and the office of the cleric they attack, and they appear to attack the former rather than the latter. But repeated attacks upon the person holding an office may weaken the office itself. Thus prolonged anti-clericalism can lead to anti-religious sentiment, or at least prepare the way for it. This, I feel, has happened in the case of the festa partiti.

In challenging the decisions of the Church relating to matters of festa policy a festa partisan often resorts to violence. He frightens the priest with home-made bombs to show his displeasure, to try and change the decision and even to compel him to leave the village. But he never attacks the ultimate right of the Church or its ministers to make those decisions. Indeed, some friends in Farruġ were quite shocked when I suggested that they were doing just this. On the other hand, this constant rebellion against the authority of the Church has accustomed people to being at odds for long periods with their parish priests as well as with the Archbishop. During these times, they often ignore what the Church has to say if it does not agree with the point of view they hold. This is the accepted pattern of behaviour, not only in villages divided by festa partiti, but also in others which have disputes with the Church. But it is only in the villages with festa partiti that these disputes, and the related anti-clerical action, take place on a regularly recurring basis. In these villages, though people are devout in observing many details of their religion, constant opposition to the parish priest in matters connected with festas has led them to look upon a measure of anti-clericalism as part of their way of life.

The relative lack of respect for the clergy in these villages has been partly responsible for a rather high turnover of parish priests. It has been shown how uncomfortable festa partiti can make the life of a parish priest. This, plus the meagre living in the smaller parishes, prompts priests to look for openings in wealthier and less troublesome villages. The Church itself regards the small rural parishes as training or 'stepping-stone parishes', as a monsignor from the Curia once described them to me. But even as such, they are unpopular, and the Archbishop often has difficulty finding priests willing to take charge of them. Farruġ, for example, has had six parish priests since 1953. The lack of continuity of Church leadership in these small, divided villages has tended to weaken its influence there and to foster a lack of respect for its authority.

In this social climate the anti-clericalism of the Labour Party fits without great difficulty. Labour supporters have already had experience as festa partisans in ignoring the commands of the Church, and in enduring the taunts and disapproval of their rivals in the other partit. For them anti-clericalism is nothing new, and they are thus not as vulnerable to public opinion and the sanctions of the Church as persons in villages which do not have this tradition of opposition to the Church.

But if there is a certain similarity between the anti-clerical behaviour of many festa enthusiasts and that of MLP supporters, most persons make a distinction between the two. The anti-clerical actions of the festa partiti are usually directed against particular clerics in connection with specific decisions. In contrast, the anti-clericalism of the Labour Party is directed at the Archbishop in particular and often at all priests in general. This difference stems from the fact that basically their challenge to the authority of the Church differs significantly. Where the festa partisan does not rationalize the distinction he makes between the person and the office of the cleric he attacks, though his behaviour shows that he does make one, the Labour supporter often proclaims that he makes such a distinction, when in fact he does not. The MLP not only challenges the statements of the Archbishop which apply to the political scene, but often questions his right to make them. This explains the difference in the reaction of the Church to the two forms of anti-clericalism.

I have suggested that the one prepares the way for the other. The rebellious atmosphere created by the disputes between the festa partiti is, I believe, as important a factor as occupational class in explaining the relatively high degree of open support the Labour Party has in the southern villages. The extent of this support, especially in the smaller villages, in spite of the sanctions of the Church, came as a surprise to some of the leaders of the MLP, who had always thought of them as dominated by their parish priests, like the small villages in Gozo. But in the spring of 1961, the small villages of Kirkop, Dingli and Gudja were placed first, second and third in an MLP competition to find the community which had the greatest proportion of new Party members. I suggest that the support for the MLP in these three villages is due not so much to their proportion of industrial labourers, which in any case is not particularly high (23, 20 and 35 per cent respectively),[1] as to their strong tradition of rebellion against the authority of the Church. Kirkop and Gudja both have active festa partiti of long standing, and while Dingli has no festa partiti now, the village has a long history of opposition to its parish priests. For example, shortly after the First World War, the Dingli Social Club had an argument with the parish priest, and for many years after, members celebrated the national feast on 8 September, instead of the patronal feast of the Assumption, simply to annoy him.

V

But whatever complex and diverse reasons people have for taking sides, the division has given rise to conflict in most villages. In this respect Kortin is no different, as the slogans displayed during the battle of the blackboards indicated. The division has cut right

[1] 1957 Census: Report on Economic Activities, pp. 41-2.

across the village and the clubs, and has brought about conflict within many families. People lament the change that has come over the village as a result. An old bachelor friend often used to complain that had we come to live there just a few years ago, 'before politics came and spoiled everything', we would have found the village a far happier place. Picnics and outings were more frequent then, and groups of friends used to gather on hot summer evenings and stroll outside the village to play guitars and sing the lilting Maltese *ghana* in the cool air away from the houses. There was also more life in the clubs. Both the Social Club and the Band Club used to take part in the national carnival competition for the best decorated carts and costumed companies. But as the political conflict has divided the island's carnival celebration in two, so it has also affected the clubs. They now celebrate neither the government's carnival nor that of the MLP for fear the question of which one to participate in would provoke a fight that would cripple the club.

Dun Bert, the parish priest in Kortin, is of course the head of the local group which supports the Archbishop and opposes the MLP. His chief lieutenants in the fight are the local clergy and the lay leaders of the religious associations. Pawlu and Anton, his two faithful helpers, are also vocal partisans, as is old Manwel. Dr. Farrugia, old Manwel's son, as a former member of the Legislative Assembly (MLA) and a leading member of one of the political parties opposed to the MLP, also belongs to the pro-Church division in the village, though he takes little part in its day-to-day affairs. The main activity and support comes from the leaders of the lay associations, especially of the Young Christian Workers, the MUSEUM and the Sodality of Our Lady. These all meet regularly in their respective premises. Many of the others, older men, spend much of their free time in Kelinu's café. These include old Manwel, Pawlu, Anton, the sacristan, the organist, and Dun Mikiel and Dun Filip, respectively the chaplains of the female and male sections of Catholic Action. This café, located right next to Dr. Farrugia's house, is the nicest café on the square, or in the village for that matter. It is the only one which the clergy, the teachers and occasionally Dr. Farrugia himself, frequent. It is thus the headquarters of the more influential village citizens who support the Archbishop. Most MLP supporters have stopped going to it, although a few still play cards there for an hour or so in the late

afternoon when they return from work. Many Labour sympathizers believe that the important anti-Labour demonstrations
and moves are plotted at Kelinu's.

The headquarters of the MLP group is the Labour Club, which is
situated just off the square and around the corner from Kelinu's.
Salvu, the ex-MLA who is the leader of the village Labour group,
spends his evenings there with his lieutenants, the officers of the
village Labour Committee. Salvu, a small building contractor, has
had little formal education, but he has an engaging personality, a
quick mind and is a persuasive speaker. He is also an excellent
comic actor, a playwright of sorts, and the author of most of the
slogans that appear on the club's blackboard. Smaller groups of
Labour supporters meet at one of the other cafés on the square,
and at some of the wine shops near the chapel of St. Paul in the
poorer section of the village. Other groups of pro-Labour friends
often gather on the steps of the church or around a bench near the
Labour club. They rarely go into the club itself, for all are
anxious to avoid being marked as open Labour supporters by the
village, which, generally speaking, is strongly anti-Labour.

The supporters of the Archbishop and those of the Labour
Party rarely meet face to face as organized bodies. When they do,
it is the occasion for a good deal of ill-feeling and, sometimes, open
hostility. This occurs when a big rally is organized in the village.
Two such rallies were held in Kortin while we were living there.
The first was on the occasion of a visit of the Archbishop; the
second was a national MLP meeting. Dun Bert and his assistants
organized a huge demonstration in honour of the Archbishop
during his visit. It was a great success. The Labour club arranged
a social and musical gathering the evening before to work up
Party solidarity, but it closed its doors during the actual visit and
cleaned off its blackboard in order not to provoke incidents. With
but one exception, there were no incidents to spoil the enthusiastic
welcome the villagers accorded the Archbishop. Many Labour
supporters attended the demonstration, for the Archbishop was
visiting the village as head of the Church in Malta to bestow the
sacrament of confirmation on the children. But as the Archbishop
and his excited escort approached the church, a bitter Labour
supporter made an insulting gesture at him. (People were quick
to inform us that the man was an outsider married into the
village.) He was subsequently arrested and convicted, for as

already noted, in Malta, it is a criminal offence to insult a minister of religion. There were no other disturbances.

The Labour rally was rather a different story. The leader of the MLP and the thousands of his supporters who came to Kortin to hear him speak received a decidedly hostile reception. Though Dun Bert did not organize a counter-demonstration for the occasion, he did arrange a mass protest meeting the evening before. The following day rival groups were out decorating. A number of MUSEUM lads under the direction of one of the older members pasted anti-MLP slogans all over the façade of the church. At the same time, a group of men were busy hanging posters and flags from the Labour club to welcome Dom Mintoff to the village.

At 4 p.m. buses and cars began to stream into the village with thousands of MLP supporters from all over the island. At about the same time the church bells began to call the faithful to a religious procession in honour of Our Lady of Fatima which Dun Bert had scheduled to take place during the Labour meeting. He himself stood in the square watching the faithful gather in the church. He also carefully observed those who passed by on their way to the Labour meeting, which was being held right behind the church. Most of the villagers who sympathized with the Labour Party but who did not support it openly did not attend the meeting. They were anxious to avoid the open break with the rest of the community which attending would have entailed. Besides, several mentioned that their confessors had told them that they would commit a mortal sin if they attended MLP meetings. All the open supporters of the MLP in the village went to the meeting.

The meeting began at about 4.30 p.m. and lasted for two hours. Shortly after it had started, Dun Bert's procession of nearly a thousand men, women and children slowly wound its way through the village and returned to the church for a period of prayer and worship. When the Labour meeting finally broke up, most of the outside supporters departed quickly, though a number were delayed because villagers had deflated the tyres of about a dozen of their cars. At this time people also began to leave the church. But the police, who were trying to keep a passage clear in the centre of the square for the stream of departing Labour supporters, kept them on the steps of the church. They waited there for a while and then began singing hymns and songs in honour of the Pope and the Archbishop, stopping now and then to shout insults at the passing Labour supporters. The square on the other side of the police cordon began to fill up with people returning from the meeting and others who left their houses to see what the excitement was about. Gradually the songs became louder and more excited, and the shouts hoarser. By then it was getting quite dark, but I could see Dun Mikiel in the front row, his hands thrust tensely into the pockets of his cassock, scowling at the passers-by while he smoked cigarette after cigarette. The tension by this time was almost electric. Suddenly, one of the local MLP supporters returning to the Labour club replied to a taunt by making a threatening gesture. The crowd in front of the church booed him loudly and surged forward. The police, anxious to hurry the trouble-maker off the square, pushed him a bit too hard and he stumbled and fell. This angered the crowd on the other side of the square and it began to press through the police cordon. At this point police reinforcements arrived and cleared the square in a few moments. Their prompt action prevented an ugly situation from going further, for there had been well over a thousand angry people facing each other, separated by less than two dozen unarmed policemen.

Four days after the meeting, Dun Bert organized a pilgrimage of reparation to atone for the insults of the MLP speakers. The procession of some 1,200 people reciting the Rosary escorted the statue of Our Lady of Sorrows through the area behind the church where the Labour meeting had been held. About 400 of the participants were outsiders who had come to Kortin from other parts of the island for the occasion. After the procession the crowd gathered in front of the church where a Mass was said. A noted Jesuit orator then rebutted the MLP speeches point by point. The whole affair had almost passed off without incident when a number of stones and bottles were thrown from behind walls at the buses and cars leaving the village.

But if there are relatively few face-to-face meetings of this kind in Kortin or elsewhere, there are many disputes that divide and weaken the clubs and associations. This matter has particularly affected Sur Ġorġ, the president of the Social Club, who feels responsible for preserving its unity in these difficult times. In Kelinu's, where many of the influential regulars are members of the Social Club, they say that it has become a Mintoff stronghold.

Many of them have stopped going there. In point of fact, Sur Ġorġ and the secretary are strongly opposed to the Labour Party, though many of the younger men and some of the most active older members support it. A number of people living nearby have complained that members praise Mintoff in loud voices. There is growing pressure on Sur Ġorġ to ban all political conversation there. He has so far resisted the pressure, for he believes that if he were to give in, he would drive away the very members who form the backbone of the club. His chief problem, as he described it to me, is how to focus the attention of the members on something other than politics. He is therefore doing his best to obtain the permits necessary to open the theatre for which they have been planning and saving for years. He feels that in the excitement of building, the members will forget their political differences and re-unite, and thus the club will pass safely through this crisis. But the permits have been slow in coming and meanwhile the pressure on him is building up. Two important members of the committee have already resigned, 'under the influence of those busy-bodies in Kelinu's', as some members described it.

The men in charge of the St. Martin Band Club in Farruġ face much the same problem. As has already been noted, most of the leaders of the two political blocs in the village are members of the St. Martin club, and several of them are on its committee. This difference of political loyalty often provokes quarrels over matters of policy. During the centenary, for example, the committee were sharply divided over whether to salute the Archbishop with the customary barrage of fireworks when he entered the village to take part in the ceremony. The matter was put to a vote, and the MLP faction won. The disgruntled losers began talking about firing off their own salute of welcome. But the crisis that this action would have brought about was avoided when the Vicar-General officiated in place of the Archbishop, who was indis-posed. As the MLP supporters had nothing against him, he received the full barrage of aerial bombs and fire crackers. The rift was thus healed, and all joined in to celebrate a rousing feast.

The following year the festa again brought a crisis with it. This time it was a far more serious one. Most of the young Labour supporters, in retaliation for the way the Church had attacked their party and its leaders, flatly refused to have anything to do with the feast. These young men included virtually all the partit's fireworkers, and without their expert help it was feared that the feast would be a miserable failure. Many Labour supporters also instructed their parents and wives not to contribute money to the feast. This depressing state of affairs continued for some time.

Then one day, about three months before the festa, Pietru, the young schoolteacher who is head of Catholic Action and treasurer of the St. Martin club, came up to me looking very pleased. He said that the feast was saved. Several events had combined to work up interest in it. It seems that most of the people had attended a large and very successful titular festa in a neighbouring village; the St. Roque fireworkers had shot off three extremely well-made test rockets; and he himself had played his tape recording of the St. Martin hymn, the anthem of the partit, over a loud-speaker in the square. These events revived interest in the festa and in the reputation of the partit. Immediately afterwards the secretary of the club, a Labour supporter who has set politics aside for the honour of the partit, called a committee meeting to discuss the problem of making fireworks. After several speeches urging members to keep their politics from spoiling the feast, the committee voted to make fireworks. Though two skilled fire-workers crossed the floor and agreed to help, none of the many experts among the rank and file followed suit. But soon after this political loyalty again began to smother the rekindled partit spirit, and one of the fireworkers all but dropped out. Moreover, Pietru, who is the village's most eloquent and outspoken enemy of the Labour Party, began to preach so vehemently to those he calls the 'lost sheep' of the club, that he antagonized many. His fund-raising suffered as a result.

About a month after this I met Toni at a festa in a neighbouring village, and we had a long talk away from the interested eyes and ears of Farruġ. Toni has been a member of the St. Martin Club committee for nearly twenty years, and until some months ago had been vice president. He was clearly very worried about the club. People were already beginning to draw parallels between the present situation and the events that led up to the split in 1930. He said he was doing his best to discourage such talk, and had now begun working hard to avoid an open break.

He pointed out that he had experienced many crises in the partit and favoured a less blunt approach to winning back the interest of the MLP members than did the crusading Pietru. He felt that he had already had some success wooing members back on a personal basis by talking only of the honour of the partit and leaving politics out altogether. He stressed that the main problem was not so much the feast but the survival of the club. 'If we can just weather out the storm until after the election we can save it.' He went on to describe how it had taken years to heal the division after the seceding Strickland supporters had rejoined in 1935. 'We must avoid a split at all costs, and the only way we can do that is to bury our political differences.' His technique for doing this was to have as few formal committee meetings as possible, to avoid discussing controversial subjects and to vote in secret, for in these times 'an open vote divides the members'.

The wise counsel and efforts of the older members, who have set politics aside, has so far kept the younger hot-heads from splitting the club. In spite of all the obstacles in its way, the feast of St. Martin turned out to be a good show. Though many supporters did not contribute, others gave more than usual and there were enough funds for a good feast. About a dozen boys worked under the direction of the two adult fireworkers, and made most of the fireworks. They gave a very good account of themselves, though not one of them is old enough (18) to join the club as a formal member. All are Catholic Action members. In fact, except for a few St. Roque boys, they are the only ones left in the society. The Catholic Action group once numbered almost fifty. The others, the sons of Labour families, had been forced out by the vote of loyalty to the Archbishop which the association's national headquarters had demanded. But their enthusiasm could not quite make up for their youth or their lack of numbers. During the Friday demonstration for the saint some outsiders who were supporters of the guest band had to help them carry the statue of their patron part of the way. This was a great comedown from the previous year, when his followers were so numerous that they had to struggle for a turn to carry him. But the noise and the gay atmosphere of the celebration rekindled the interest of a number of the Labour supporters. Several helped to erect the decorations on Saturday; a few even joined in one of the band marches.

VI

It is of course an open question how much longer the intense partit spirit can survive in the face of the political division now cutting across all festa partiti. In Farruġ the division between the festa partiti, such a strong force in the past, is now of less importance as a principle of social organization than the rivalry between the supporters and opponents of the MLP. The relative importance in Farruġ, as everywhere, of this latter division is directly related to the intensity of the conflict at the national level between the MLP and the Church. If it decreases, so will that at the village level. But the longer it lasts, the more difficult it will be to remove it completely from the social scene. Both the Church and the Labour Party, through their respective societies, committees and social clubs, are building up an institutional framework that is incorporating this political opposition on a permanent basis in all villages. This is taking place in much the same way as the confraternities and social clubs a hundred years ago made permanent the conflict between rival factions competing over the celebration of saints.

The rivalry between the Church and the MLP, as well as that between competing political parties, reflects the increasing involvement of the villager in the political life of his country. It was perhaps only due to Malta's peculiar position as a colony and an island fortress, a role which effectively prevented the development of an active internal political life of the more conventional kind, that competition over church privileges and saints was able to assume the importance it has. It is not surprising that the changing nature of Malta's strategic and constitutional position should alter the tempo and character of its internal political life. In the villages, this change is reflected in the weakening of the festa partiti by national political issues.

CHAPTER VIII

The Village and the Outside World

Every Maltese is at the centre of a large network of kin relations. Thus, when the need arises, many people are able to move along the intricate channels of consanguinity and affinity to establish personal contact with influential persons. It has also been noted that this network of kin can be extended artificially. Important persons, such as politicians, police officers, high civil servants and professionals are often invited to become godparents, marriage witnesses and confirmation sponsors. These relationships are constantly manipulated to bring individuals in touch with decision makers. This gives a personal content to many official decisions. Since most people honour the obligations of kinship, friendship and neighbourhood, requests which appeal to these values stand a good chance of a favourable reply. But a large network of kinsmen can also be a liability to a civil servant, for the favourable treatment he is expected to give a kinsman often conflicts with the civil service ethic of impartiality. This can place persons in authority in awkward positions, since the refusal of a request may seriously affect either their personal relations or their professional integrity. Maltese civil servants thus work under pressure which is quite unfamiliar to their counterparts in larger, less intimately related societies.

II

Another method of handling contacts with authority is through influential patrons. By 'patron' I mean a person who uses his influence to assist and protect some other person, who then becomes his 'client'. In a Catholic society there is a strong ideological basis for a system of patronage, for there is great similarity between the function of saints and mortal patrons. Michael Kenny points to this correspondence in his study of patronage in Spain[1] and, in general terms, his analysis is equally applicable to

[1] 'Patterns of Patronage in Spain', *Anthropological Quarterly*, XXXIII (January 1960), pp. 14–23.

Malta. He sees the patronage system in Spain as a pyramidal structure incorporating both the natural and the spiritual worlds. At the top is God, the supreme patron who is not dependent upon anyone. At the base are the persons who have no clients. Between these lowly clients and God there are many different ranks of patrons, each of whom has his own small pyramid of clients. They, in turn, are clients dependent upon other higher and more influential persons. The patrons of each rank form a group which asks favours from one another on behalf of their clients.

The intermediaries between man and God are the saints, who are closer to God than man is. A person who seeks to influence the decision of a higher authority similarly looks for a person who, by virtue of his kin relation or social position, is closer to the decision maker than he. In view of the functional similarity of saints to living patrons, it should not come as a surprise that the word for patron in Maltese is 'saint' (*qaddis*; plural *qaddisin*). Several proverbs underline the important role that patrons play in Maltese social life. Here are two: 'Without saints you can't get to heaven' (*Minghajr qaddisin ma titlax il-genna*); and 'You can do nothing without saints' (*Minghajr qaddisin ma taghmel xejn*). Another points to the fact that any patron-client relationship is not without obligation, even danger, for the client: 'He who fattens you will kill you' (*Min semmnek joqtlok*).

Who are these 'saints', these men of influence? For the most part they are people who have already been encountered, albeit in a slightly different capacity. They are the professionals, the civil servants and, in general, the wealthy and powerful. They are persons, respected for their education and social standing in the world outside the village, who can deal as equals with other important people and decision-makers, many of whom are their relatives and former classmates. Their patronage is sought by individuals and groups alike. They are often asked to become god-parents, and they are called on to handle the ceremonial, business and political relations of clubs. They are also called on to help secure employment, building permits, hawkers licences or a long-delayed hearing at the law courts. Generally speaking, villagers choose patrons from the circle of influential people with whom they have the closest contact: the local professionals, the parish priest and clergy, the important landlords, all of whom command respect outside the village. Some clients are related to their patrons; others have established fairly close contact with them through business relations.

The patronage of the parish priest has traditionally been important. Not only are all villagers his spiritual clients, but he is also a source of charity and assistance in many fields. He serves his parishioners individually in the capacity of legal adviser, character reference and often also as letter-writer and banker. He frequently argues their claims against the government. He also represents the interests of the community at large, and attempts, often successfully, to obtain improved public amenities such as new roads, street lighting and so on. At least, this is the role that he occupied until the introduction of representative government.

III

Influence through the networks of personal relations and patrons is the traditional method of handling contacts with authority. It still operates when representative government is in abeyance. But the advent of elected government introduced a new set of relations, and provided a new focus of power. Political parties and professional politicians provided new and surer channels of influence and sources of patronage, though they have not replaced the old ones. The villager now uses both old and new channels, separately or together.

The organization of all parties, at least before Mintoff reorganized the Labour Party, was rather simple. Party interests were represented in the villages by personal canvassers or party agents, as well as by the candidates themselves. The old Labour Party under Paul Boffa had a number of village party committees. When the party was returned to power, patronage and influence flowed abundantly, and brought the whole structure into vigorous life. The canvassers became important people who could pass along requests and schedule appointments with the local MLA's and even the Ministers. They also helped the local MLA's prepare the lists of people who were to be given jobs, for until 1955 most of the lower-grade industrial labourers with the Public Works Department were employed upon the recommendation of the local MLA's. Politicians who held office before 1955 often told me that making out the employment rosters and dealing with the daily queue of job-seekers were among their most difficult and time-consuming tasks. To help as many as possible, they often made up new job rosters every few months.

Canvassers would often expect presents for their work as intermediaries and for the favours they promised or secured. By and large, the party agents or canvassers were not popular figures, at least in retrospect. I came across many accounts of how they had exploited their positions to enrich themselves. The usual story was that they had accepted gifts – a rabbit, some chickens, a bottle of whisky or even cash – but had not assisted as they had promised. These tales may or may not be true; I had no way of checking. It is significant, however, that persons of all political colours, including former Ministers and MLA's, believe them to be true.

Mintoff's government did much to change the course of the stream of political patronage. To begin with, shortly after it came into office in 1955, the MLP passed a law which made it compulsory for those seeking employment with the government as industrial labourers to register with the Department of Emigration, Labour and Social Welfare.[1] There they had to wait their turn. This took away from MLA's a considerable source of patronage. The MLP also established special sub-committees of the Labour Committees in each village to deal with the complaints and requests of the local inhabitants. A member of the sub-committee was generally available to the public for an hour or two every evening. All requests for assistance and complaints were discussed by the entire sub-committee, which would countersign the routine ones and send them along to the appropriate government department. More important matters were brought personally to the attention of the civil servant concerned by a member of the sub-committee. Complicated requests and serious complaints were forwarded to the District Committee, where they were discussed at the regular weekly meetings with the district MLA's, who might then take the matter up directly with the Minister. Civil servants, on the whole, handled complaints and requests for action from the Local Committees with much the same dispatch they would give a request from their Minister. Some Ministers even went so far as to instruct their Department Heads to ignore all complaints brought to them by private persons, especially parish priests. They were told only to act on those presented by the Local Committee.

[1] Act No. XIV, 1955: 'An Act to Make Provisions for the Establishment and Regulation of an Employment Service.'

10

Another very important function the Local Committees performed during the period the MLP was in power was to obtain improvements for the village. Requests for drainage, new roads, street lighting and, above all, new schools, were submitted to the District Committees. There the proposals were screened and given priority ratings by the committee members and the district MLA's. When these projects were implemented, and a large number were, the Local Committees naturally received credit for them. This added to their claim to represent their villages, and strengthened the formal structure of the party.

This system of handling patronage and complaints gave the villager a direct contact with authority. It was a fairly simple procedure, and many considered it reasonably impartial, though of course it did help to be a member of the Labour Party in good standing. Moreover, the complainant, even though he might not succeed in his cause, had the satisfaction that it had received attention, and it did not cost him a nice fat rabbit. This does not mean that there was no abuse. Civil servants complained that they were often intimidated by zealous MLP members who threatened to report them to their Ministers if they did not comply as requested. This friction was particularly keen between the Local Committee members and the village police, street sweepers and teachers. One head teacher I knew was particularly bitter about his caretaker, who was a member of the village MLP committee. The caretaker would stroll into the head teacher's office if he disagreed with the disciplining of a child, for example, and threaten to report him to the Minister if he did not lighten the punishment.

But on the whole, the MLP made a concerted effort to take patronage out of the hands of canvassers and MLA's alike and channel it through the various committees of the party apparatus. This not only strengthened the party, it also won it considerable popularity. Moreover, it relieved MLA's and Ministers of a heavy administrative load; they were only called in on the more complicated matters. In short, the Local Committees came to function as branches of the government.

When the Labour Government resigned in 1958, the MLP clubs and committees lost the influence they had with government. They once more became merely propaganda and social centres. But the role they had played for three years in representing the interests of government at the village level and in forwarding the requests and complaints of the villagers to government had greatly increased their strength, and that of the party they represented. As the members operated as a formal committee and not as individuals, they had the esteem and respect of most of the community. They also had considerable power in local affairs. In fact, for three years the leaders of the Labour group in the village ranked alongside the parish priest and the professionals as the most prominent and influential citizens of the village. The canvassers of the rival parties had perhaps had power, but they had never had respect. Theirs was always rather an underhanded operation, that was often disowned by MLA's when they were confronted with it. The MLP, on the other hand, delegated responsibility to Local Committees, and the Ministers legitimized them by openly working through them in all their relations with the villages. Villagers were also openly encouraged to work through them. These committees thus served the ends of the Labour Party most successfully. It is quite likely, therefore, that in the future other parties will find it politically as well as administratively expedient to develop and work through village committees patterned on the model so successfully tested by the Labour Party.

The party system has come into direct conflict with the traditional relations between patron and client at relatively few points. This is largely because most patrons who desired to were able to move successfully into the new field of party politics. A notable exception are priests, who are no longer permitted by their Bishops to stand for national political office. Their power to influence authority has thus been weakened by the new source of patronage and influence open to their parishioners. In particular, parish priests came into open conflict with the village MLP committees during the Labour Party's time in power after 1955. Not surprisingly, their clash at the village level mirrored the dispute between the Archbishop and the MLP at the national level. That is, it was a conflict between the religious authority of the Church and the secular authority of the State, represented in the villages by the Local Committees of the Labour Party. Both the parish priest and the Local Committee claimed to represent the village, and both sought by mobilizing their supporters to advance their claim at the expense of their opponents. This invariably resulted in a struggle for power during which the Labour supporters were accused of being anti-clerical and against the Church because they opposed the will of the parish priest.

Shortly after Mintoff took office, the Local Committee in Kortin made plans to open a new avenue into the village. The scheme, first projected by government planners over sixty years before, was designed to ease the flow of traffic through the village and provide a wide, tree-lined promenade leading to the main square in front of the church. Unfortunately, the project required the demolition of four buildings, two of which were small chapels used as warehouses for the festa decorations. Because of this Dun Bert, the parish priest, bitterly opposed the scheme, as had his predecessors. He claimed that most of the village supported him. The Labour Committee, on the other hand, felt that it had the backing of the village, and went ahead with the project. The road was finally opened, and it proved to be a great success. But the two small churches were destroyed, and the relations between the Labour group and the parish priest remained hostile. Six years later, Dun Bert and his supporters were still pointing to the avenue as positive proof that the Labour Party is fundamentally opposed to the Church.

IV

But if the political parties have modified the traditional system of patronage somewhat by providing a new channel of influence for the villager, the professional politician of today is by and large the same traditional patron. That is, the successful politicians are largely drawn from the professional classes; they are still the doctors, the lawyers, the architects and the chemists. Indeed, until recently the lists of candidates often read like directories of the professional classes. This situation prevailed until about the time of the Labour Party split in 1949, when virtually all the professional class Labour MLA's sided with Dr. Boffa and formed the Workers' Party, while most of the MLP Executive and the rank and file supported Mintoff. After this the Labour Party asked people from all classes to stand as candidates, and began to push up working-class leaders trained in union and club politics. But the politicians from the professional class still heavily outnumber their working-class colleagues, even in the Labour Party.

Table 8 below illustrates this. Of the fifty MLA's elected in the

1962 elections, three-fourths are members of the professional classes. The remainder are persons who, for the most part, have risen to positions of influence through party and trade union hierarchies.

TABLE 8. Occupation of Candidates Elected to the 1962 Malta Legislative Assembly

OCCUPATION	POLITICAL PARTY				
	Nationalist	Labour	Other	Total	Percentage
Professional	24	9	5	38	76
Administrative	1	4	2	7	14
Skilled Labour	—	3	2	5	10
Total	25	16	9	50	100

The way a political candidate recruits a following depends upon his status and party. All candidates recruit support through their relatives and friends; and all usually have a following in their own villages outside this circle of relatives. To get this, they must usually be successful politicians at the village level. It is for this reason that so many politicians are also presidents of local band and social clubs, and even of some of the lay apostolate societies. Next, every candidate must establish contact with the people in his electoral district outside the village. Since there are usually at least five candidates from each party standing in every district, each normally concentrates his campaign on one part of the district. He does this by making frequent rounds of all the band and social clubs and important wine shops in his territory. There he listens to complaints and requests and, in general, tries to establish a reputation as a generous and approachable person without committing himself to do specific favours. But above all, it is important for him to meet many people, for the Maltese voter does not like to give his first vote to a person he, or at least some member of his immediate family, does not know personally. Finally, all candidates tour their districts just before the election and make speeches.

Candidates who are doctors, lawyers, notaries, architects and so on, have a decided advantage. As professionals, they already have close personal contact with a large number of clients, many of whom are bound to them by debts, or obligated to them for help and favours. These obligations are important, for the Maltese villager does not like to receive something for nothing, and he does not rest easily until he has repaid it. This is as true of corporate groups such as the band clubs as it is of individuals Frequently the financial circumstances of the client, or the very nature of the favour, make it difficult or impossible for him to meet his obligation. His vote, and those of his family, provide the logical and accepted means to this end. This extends the relationship between patron and client to include that between politician and constituent.

Candidates who do not have the professional qualifications or high status necessary to recruit a following in this way are at a disadvantage. This is especially true for many of the Labour Party candidates, whose education and social standing at times compare unfavourably with those of their rivals. It was principally to overcome this handicap that the Labour Party sought to strengthen the party at the expense of individual candidates. It did this by limiting the system of political patronage which prevailed under previous governments and curbing the influence of the canvassers. In fact, the MLP officially forbade its candidates to employ canvassers. (Though, of course, many candidates have informal canvassers in their friends, relatives and clients.) At the same time, the party directed its propaganda at building up the image of the party and its leader. Labour supporters were constantly urged to vote for the party and not for individuals. By and large its campaign has been most successful. Its sympathizers not only vote for candidates who do not conform to the traditional image of the professional patron-politician, but they also vote across class lines, i.e. the teacher voting for an ex-dockyard fitter.

All candidates have to take into account the parochial rivalries which often cut across their districts. This is particularly true of the rivalry between the festa partiti. It has been noted that there is often a political polarity between festa partiti in the same village, and that sometimes the rivalry is so strong that partisans vote against a political party simply because a leading member of the rival partit is a candidate for it. But the number of people who place loyalty to their festa partit before support of a political party is declining. Nonetheless, if parochial rivalry no longer determines which party will get the votes, it very often decides which of the candidates within the party will. Many people have assured me that it is almost unheard of for a member of a festa partit to vote for a member of the rival partit, even though both support the same political party. Thus a politician who is also a leading member of a festa partit always asks a rival candidate from his party to come to his village and canvass the party votes from the opposite festa partit.

Most people believe that politicians trade promises to assist festa partiti in return for votes. One well-known Labour politician who is the leader of the secondary festa partit in his own village, made such a promise to gain the support of a neighbouring secondary partit that was facing eviction. In return for the votes of the partit, he offered to introduce a bill into the Legislative Assembly which would prevent landlords from evicting band clubs. The proposition appealed to the partit and the bill, which gained a great deal of support for the Labour Party from other clubs as well, became law.[1] In fact, it was one of the first laws the MLP enacted after it was returned to office in 1955. Partly as a result of his promise of assistance, but also because of his keen interest in the problems of secondary festa partiti, this candidate became so identified with this neighbouring partit that he had to ask MLP candidates from the other side of the electoral district to bid for the Labour votes of the members of the opposite partit. He naturally asked them to canvass the Labour votes of the titular partit in his own village as well.

But perhaps the most famous case of this kind, and certainly the most conspicuous, took place in Gozo. For many years the supporters of the Leone partit in Rabat had been embarrassed by the fact that the statue of their beloved patron could not be taken in processions from the cathedral. There was simply no way for her to pass through the walls of the old citadel in which the cathedral was situated. The members of the partit wished to remedy this by breaching the wall and making a large gate, but the Antiquities Board strongly opposed the idea. Finally, an ambitious MLP candidate came to their rescue. He is alleged to have promised them help if they voted for him. Whether the deal for votes is true I do not know. I do know, however, that the politician was elected and succeeded in having a huge new gate torn in the historic citadel. That he did this at public expense, against the orders of his Ministers and in defiance of the Antiquities Board, is evidence of his ingenuity and single-mindedness. Of course, it might also have

---

[1] Act V, 1955: 'An Act to Amend the Reletting of Urban Property (Regulation) Ordinance.'

been due to the amount of pressure that the partit brought to bear on him.

V

But popularity, close contact with the electorate and the support of his party and festa partit are not always enough to assure the success of a candidate. In order to understand why this is so, it is necessary to examine the electoral process. The system of voting which has been used in Malta since 1921 is proportional representation with the single transferable vote. The country is divided into ten electoral districts, each of which returns five representatives to the Legislative Assembly. The districts are based on population density, and each averages about 15,000 registered voters. A candidate need not be resident in a district in order to stand for election there, and he can stand in two districts at the same time. If he is successful in both, he relinquishes one seat, which is then filled by a member of his party chosen in a by-election. At the polling booth each voter is given a ballot paper listing all the candidates standing in the district, and is required to rank them by placing a number against the name of each, to indicate the order of preference. After the polling is finished, all the ballot boxes from a district are opened simultaneously and the ballot papers mixed. The votes are then counted. As each paper is opened, a single vote is credited to the candidate to whom the voter has given first preference. This is the first count. A candidate is declared elected if he receives a certain proportion of the total number of votes cast.[1] After the first count the candidate with the lowest number of votes is eliminated, and his votes are redistributed in accordance with the second preferences. The votes are then retotalled for the second count. The candidate with the lowest number of votes is again eliminated, and his votes are redistributed for the third count. The elimination of candidates and the redistribution of their votes continues until five candidates receive the required quota of votes.

Few candidates are elected on the first count, for the first preferences of the voters are generally distributed among a large number. First preferences reflect the popularity of a candidate and the size of his following, but the secondary votes he receives are

---

[1] This quota, the Droop quota, is one plus the total number of votes cast, divided by the number of seats (5) plus one.

critical to his election. Successful politicians repeatedly stressed to me the importance of carefully cultivating secondary preferences. As one put it, 'The first preferences keep you from being eliminated, but the secondary ones elect you.' The votes a candidate gets on subsequent counts are the result of his ability (i) to bargain with other candidates for the secondary preferences of their followers, and (ii) to set up a network of personal canvassers to secure these secondary preferences from the supporters of candidates who do not wish to release them to him. One technique that all candidates use is to encourage popular village figures to stand as mock candidates for vote-getting purposes. The understanding is that the politician is to receive their secondary preferences if they are defeated, as they usually are, since they are not generally known outside their villages. In exchange for these votes, the professional politician generally offers to pay the mock candidate's election expenses, or if elected to procure some favour for him, or both. This technique has resulted in an extraordinary number of candidates contesting every election. In 1955 a total of 140 candidates from three parties contested 40 seats; in 1962 there were 302 for six parties and 50 seats. Thus voters, many of whom are illiterate, are faced with a bewildering choice of candidates arranged alphabetically on ballots that are sometimes three feet long.

Another way for a candidate to gather secondary votes is to exchange secondary preferences with a rival. Occasionally a candidate tries to play both ends against the middle. That is, he promises his second votes to more than one of his rivals in exchange for theirs. This works very well for him if his rivals are eliminated before he is, but if he goes first, the official record of the distribution of his votes soon shows up his duplicity.

While this system of voting assures representation to all shades of political opinion, it works in several ways against the development of a strong two-party system. To begin with, it is ideally suited to the needs of the traditional patron-politician with his own localized, semi-private political organization of canvassers, mock candidates and clients. The present system of voting in combination with this organization assures him that many votes will be funnelled in to him. In the past these personal organizations ensured the re-election of politicians even if they changed parties. In fact a politician's supporters sometimes encourage him to switch to the party with best chance of success, for they know that if he is elected, he will channel patronage to them, often at the expense of the rest of his electoral district.

This system of voting also encourages contests between candidates from the same party. Such contests, carried out in public and in the heat of a campaign, often create hostility among the leaders of the party, and weaken its solidarity.

Finally, because this proportional system makes it possible for popular minority candidates to be elected, it encourages dissident factions to hive off from the major parties and found new ones. This seriously weakens the parent parties. Thus, although the only political division of real importance is that between the supporters of the Archbishop and those who favour Mintoff, there are now six political parties in Malta. It is not surprising therefore that the minority parties, and Miss Strickland's Progressive Constitutional Party in particular, are strongly in favour of retaining the present electoral system. Without it they would not be represented. The Malta Labour Party, which favours a strong two-party system, would prefer to see substituted an electoral system which would eliminate the smaller parties and strengthen the major parties. The Nationalist Party, although it would benefit from a change in the electoral system which would eliminate many of its rivals, has remained relatively silent on this point. This is because most of its leading members are patron-politicians of the old school. They owe their political life and the influence they command to the electoral system which has enabled them to build their own personal political organizations. The Nationalist Party is a party of respected and influential men, but in their strength lies its weakness. It is a party of politicians, rather than a politician's party. Dr. Borg Olivier, the Nationalist Prime Minister, is a first among equals; he does not lead his party in the sense that Mintoff leads the Malta Labour Party.

In short the Maltese system of proportional representation facilitates the emergence of minority parties. It also weakens the major parties by promoting intra-party rivalry and helping to keep alive the tradition of local patron-politicians. These factors militate against the development of a strong central government. It can be argued forcefully that Malta, which is facing a critical period in its economic and constitutional development, is now in greater need of a strong central government than ever before. It would therefore seem that as this need becomes more pronounced, and as the Maltese voter gains in sophistication, there will be increasing pressure to change the present system of voting to one which strengthens the national government rather than weakens it.

VI

In addition to personal kin ties, patrons, political parties and politicians, pressure groups provide yet another way by which the villager can influence authorities outside his community. By bringing interest groups from one village into contact with similar groups in other villages, they permit united action for the resolution of common problems. The band clubs and football clubs have active national associations. Village lay apostolate societies have their own national bodies as well as the Diocesan Coordinating Junta, a powerful body which has now become one of the strongest forces opposed to the MLP. In view of the important part it and the other Church societies played in defeating the Labour Party in the recent election, they will probably be able to provide a channel of contact with the Ministers and anti-Labour MLA's. Some have already begun to apply pressure to obtain playgrounds and public conveniences for their respective villages.

Even the festa partiti have their associations. The Association of Secondary Feasts works to obtain new Church privileges for its members. It is opposed by the Association of Titular Feasts, which has formally advised the Archbishop that if he grants privileges to the secondary partiti, its members will stop celebrating the titular feasts.

Finally, there are also a number of trade unions. Though most have no village level organization or representatives, and play no direct part in village politics, some, in particular the General Workers Union and the Gozo Agricultural Co-operative Society, a large proportion of whose members live in the villages, play an important part in national politics. They thus provide another channel through which persons at the village level can influence decisions at the national level.

CHAPTER IX

Conclusion

This study has been concerned with Maltese village politics. It has looked at the ways in which persons and groups compete to influence the outcome of disputes and community decisions in accordance with their own interests. In particular, it has examined the nature of the groups, the issues between them and the means by which they influenced their outcome. The various groups involved varied from parishes to political parties, and from associations to factions. The issues between them, though they also varied, all had one thing in common: in one way or another they involved the Church. Whether the competition between parishes for the title of Basilica, between festa partiti over their saints or between the supporters of Mintoff and their opponents, all were somehow related to the Church. Much of the political action we studied involved attempts to influence its decisions.

It may now be asked why the Church is so intimately involved in political activity at all levels. Part of the answer lies in history, for in the absence of any form of civil government at the village level, the Church represented the interests of the people to the secular authorities governing the islands: first to the Knights of St. John, and later to the British. Thus for centuries the Church played the important political role of defender of the interests of the people. Its importance in the political and its dominance in the religious sphere reinforced each other. It is not strange that at the village level the Church controls the outcome of many of the issues considered of importance to the community, since for centuries a village has had little corporate reality outside the religious framework. That is, it only assumes some semblance of group solidarity or unity as a parish. As a parish its inhabitants own property, meet for worship, celebrate feasts, have a collective leader in their parish priest and a common symbol and patron in their titular saint. As members of a village, considered as a community outside the structure of the Church, they have and can do none of these things. This study of village politics has thus been largely concerned with parish politics. In this field the Church is the arbiter of all issues of policy. It is therefore the authority that hands down decisions on matters which concern the community; it is also the authority against which disappointed petitioners rebel.

II

At the national level, the picture is similar. Since the Church for so long has represented the interests of a solidly Catholic people *vis-à-vis* the State, it has always exercised considerable influence, if not authority, in matters of national policy. Hence some groups have often disagreed with its decisions. Both during the late 'twenties and early 'thirties and more recently, political parties have rebelled against its authority. Their rebellions have given rise to conflicts that have divided the country.

Though the Maltese do not regard this conflict as permanent, it would seem from its recurrence during Malta's only two periods of sustained representative government that it is, in fact, inherent in the social system. That is, it has followed almost inevitably upon the introduction of elected government into a society linked as closely with the Church as Malta is. Issues of national policy, which in countries where the Church is not such an integral part of society would be regarded as purely political and devoid of religious content, in Malta become matters on which the Church feels obliged to make known its views. Disputes arise when the views of a political party differ from those held by the Church. The party then accuses the Church of interfering in politics, and is in turn charged by the Church with being anti-clerical. Political issues become religious ones, or, seen from another point of view, religious ones become political. But in the dispute which follows, people from all walks of life are forced to make a choice between Church and political party. The resulting conflict divides the islands into bitterly opposed factions.

The persistence of this conflict, of course, is partly dependent upon the continuing survival of a political party at variance with the Church. In the past this was Strickland's Constitutional Party; at present it is the Malta Labour Party; in the future it may be yet another. The conflict which divided the country thirty years ago diminished after Strickland made peace with the Church; it disappeared when the old Constitutional Party died out in the long period of Governor's rule and the war that followed. At present, however, the MLP shows no signs of weakening. On the contrary, it is as tightly united and strong today as it has ever been. Thus this conflict will in all probability continue to divide Malta and Gozo in the foreseeable future, though its intensity may fluctuate.

It is well to remember that this study was carried out at a time when the hostility between these two camps was at its peak. Some of the examples that have been given, therefore, are extreme cases which would have been quite inconceivable even ten years ago. It is also possible that ten years hence they will appear equally strange. But this does not detract from the relevance of the analysis, for if the examples given are ephemeral, the principles which they illustrate are permanent.

III

In many respects the rebellion of a political party against the authority of the Bishop is similar to that of a festa partit against its parish priest. There is an important difference, however; the festa partit can appeal an unfavourable decision of its parish priest to the Archbishop. If the latter rules against the partit, it can bring pressure to bear that may result in the transfer of the parish priest. A political party, on the other hand, cannot appeal the unfavourable decisions of the Bishop to any local authority, for in his diocese his word is law. Though in theory such disputes can be referred to the Holy See, in practice, as in the case of Strickland's conflict with the Church, they fester for so long that by the time Rome is brought in reconciliation is difficult, if not impossible. If in practice a political party cannot appeal to a higher authority, it can even less agitate for the replacement of the Bishop. Thus disputes remain unresolved and the supporters of the political party become progressively more anti-clerical. Finally, their anti-clericalism is equated with anti-Catholicism, and their rebellion against authority with revolt against the social order.

But is it in fact a revolution? It is important to draw a clear distinction between rebellion and revolution.[1] In the case of the former, people may turn against a leader personally, and may

[1] Cf. Max Gluckman, *Custom and Conflict in Africa* (Oxford, Basil Blackwell, 1959), p. 28.

even try to remove him from office. But they do not attack the office itself. In contrast, a revolution aims at changing not only the office-holder, but also the nature of the office and the social order in which it functions. Though the Malta Labour Party has strongly criticized the Archbishop and the clergy, often in insulting language, for their refusal to endorse its integration scheme, and, later, its demands for independence, it has never suggested that the office of archbishop should be abolished or the Church suppressed. The Church, however, attacks Mintoff as though he were bent on overthrowing the established social order in general, and the Catholic Church in particular. The extremely severe sanctions that it has directed against the MLP and its leaders reflect this point of view.

There is a very real danger that this strong medicine may kill the patient, for there is evidence that the MLP's anti-clericalism is in fact becoming anti-Catholicism, and the rebellion a revolt against the Church. Some of the more extreme, educated Labour supporters are showing a growing interest in the ideologies of countries which have fought successful battles against the Church. Though the great majority of the Labour supporters would still like to be devout Catholics, a small but increasing number are beginning to question the social order. As one remarked to me, 'I'm regarded as a Communist by my neighbours and the Church, which denies me its sacraments. Have I anything to lose by becoming one?' Though Communist literature rarely finds its way into Malta, since it is illegal to send it in the mails, a number of persons have begun to listen regularly to Radio Moscow. A few are even discussing the possibility of joining another church.

IV

But in spite of this bitter conflict, Maltese villages are still tightly united communities, life goes on and the social order does not disintegrate. Considering everything, there has been relatively little open violence between the supporters of the Church and the Labour Party. If occasionally there was some, it was most often caused by or directed against outsiders, either those who married into the villages, or who were imported for some special occasion from other villages. The battle between the Gozitans and the Maltese Labour supporters was an extreme case of this kind. But there have been remarkably few of the overtly hostile attacks, common when festa partiti are registering disagreement. What accounts for the qualitative difference in the violence between the groups involved in these two types of conflict? What prevents the national political conflict from degenerating into widespread violence, from destroying normal relations, thus making shambles of the social order? Is it merely the presence of a large, efficient police force?

In point of fact, there are many institutions and ties that operate to exert pressure on the opponents to reach a settlement, and so prevent the dispute from destroying the social system. The most important of the factors that inhibit the spread of conflict is the existence of persons whose loyalties are divided between the conflicting sides. Such persons have a vested interest in the maintenance of peace and limitation of the area of conflict.[1]

The considerable difference between the disputes of festa partiti with the Church, and the conflict between the Church and the Labour Party, has been stressed. The disputes involving festa partiti are localized, their course is highly formalized, there are acknowledged peace-makers: they are clearly rebellions in the sense that Gluckman uses. These disputes are also tightly circumscribed by customary safeguards which keep them from spreading and channel them through set stages until they have been resolved. It is patterned action which, in spite of its occasional violence, does not threaten the position of the Church. In contrast, the conflict between the MLP and the Church is not localized, it is not circumscribed by a body of custom which keeps it from spreading, and there are no acknowledged peace-makers who can mediate between the disputants. Not only is it inherent, it is irresoluble. There is an air of revolt about it and if it were allowed to run to the violence of some of the clashes between festa partiti and the Church, it could throw the country into civil war. The violence of the festa partiti does not threaten the social order, that between supporters of the Church and the MLP would.

What keeps the conflict from becoming more violent are the thousands of persons who have their allegiances divided between the Church and the Labour Party. All these people work to keep the conflict from spreading, if not actually to make peace. Who are they? They are the countless persons whose families have been

[1] *Ibid.*, *passim.*

divided by the conflict, the office-holders who have laid politics aside to preserve the unity of the clubs for which they are responsible, the many who have sought to avoid open commitments to either side, and to remain in contact with both. They are the people who, in spite of all that has been preached and said against them by both sides, still look to both the Archbishop and Mintoff as their leaders, the one in the religious sphere, the other in the political. They see nothing inconsistent in hanging pictures of the two side by side in their houses. All have a vested interest in peace; and all work in their own way to keep the conflict from spreading and destroying completely their customary way of life.

At one time the entire civil service worked to prevent the spread of conflict in much the same way. When the Labour Party took over the government many civil servants, forced by the nature of their office to carry out the orders of the party in power, were obliged to administer policies which were contrary to the declared interests of the Church. Their loyalties were thus often divided between the two. Some of the higher civil servants carried messages between the two sides. Others called at the Curia merely to assure the Church that they implemented unwillingly the controversial policies. Yet others acted quietly in their own various ways to reduce the tension between government and Church that made their own positions so uncomfortable. Civil servants at all levels thus worked to keep the Church and the Labour Government in touch with each other and exerted considerable pressure to prevent the relations between the two from deteriorating even more. But their conciliatory influence came to an end when the Labour Party resigned. It is not surprising, therefore, that with the removal of this bridge between the MLP and the Church, the conflict became more intense almost immediately.

The two sides are now linked together only by the many persons with conflicting allegiances. Yet their ability to keep the conflict from spreading is slowly being reduced by the uncompromising position of the Church which is forcing them to take sides openly. As these persons reluctantly do so, the important cross links that tie the two combatants together are snapped off one by one, and the conflict becomes progressively more intense.

V

What of the future? It would seem likely that the present conflict will continue. The dispute between the Church and the Labour Party has become institutionalized in many villages through their respective associations and social clubs. The major political activity at the village level will thus most likely continue to be a reflection of that at the national level. It will be a dispute between those who wish to preserve the identity of the village as a parish, with the dependence upon the Church that it implies, and the secular elements who wish to establish the village as a political unit apart from the Church. But there will also be other conflicting groups, such as the festa partiti, which will continue to manipulate this political division to their own advantage. The leader of one of the secondary festa partiti indicated to me how this may take place. He was discussing the recent attempts of the Association of Secondary Feasts to increase the scale of its members' feasts, and concluded by remarking, 'If the Archbishop doesn't increase our feast this year, ninety per cent of the club will vote for Mintoff in the coming election.' Thus in the future, as in the past, the Church will continue to be one of the central actors in the drama of Maltese village politics.

1968 Postscript

The eight years that have passed since I made the study contained in these pages, have been turbulent years for Malta. The Island's garrison economy has been shaken by the withdrawal of most of Britain's armed services' personnel and the rapid rundown of the giant naval dockyard. In the political field internal conflict has persisted, and the strife with Britain culminated in 1964 in independence. In the religious field an attempt has been made to implement some of the far-reaching changes recommended by the Second Vatican Council. Is in fact the picture I sketched of certain aspects of village life in Malta during the early sixties still valid today?

During the summer of 1967, thanks to the generosity of the Wenner-Gren Foundation for Anthropological Research, I was able to revisit Malta briefly to try and answer that question.[1]

The first thing that struck me was that Malta in 1967 appeared far more prosperous than in 1961. This was not a false impression: Malta is better off than ever before because there are more jobs for fewer people. A sharp rise in the rate of emigration, which reached a peak of almost 9,000 during 1964, reflected public concern with the uncertain economic and political future of the newly independent islands. This, combined with the steady decrease in the birth rate, brought about a decline in the population: the 1967 census showed a population of just over 314,000, almost 5,500 less than the 1957 census.

During the same period a number of new industries were established in Malta; these to some extent offset the impact of the rundown of the British military establishment. The most important of these is the tourist industry: Malta and Gozo are becoming increasingly popular tourist resorts. This has brought about feverish activity to construct accommodation to house the

[1] See also my *Hal-Farruġ: A Village in Malta* (New York: Holt, Rinehart and Winston, 1969).

short-term visitors, the foreign settlers as well as the growing number of Maltese wishing and able to spend their summers by the sea. There is now actually a shortage of labour in some areas of the construction and catering industries. Not surprisingly, the emigration rate has recently decreased sharply; it now stands well below the level of the early sixties. These new industries sparked off a wave of land speculation among foreigners as well as Maltese from all walks of life. This, in turn, has driven up the cost of living, for the average Maltese must now compete with retired British civil servants, ex-Rhodesian planters, wealthy continental sun-seekers and hotel combines for houses and building sites. The speculation continues largely unchecked, possibly because influential members of government, opposition and administration have growing vested interests in the expanding property market and construction industry.

The rise in the cost of living has been partly compensated by a slight increase in wage rates and, more significantly, an increase in the employment possibilities for village women. In Farruġ, for example, the number of women working had risen from 60 in 1960 to 118 by 1967. Most are unmarried and under 20. Eight out of ten work outside the village: no less than 40 are maids, mostly in the Sliema area. This has meant that there is more money than ever circulating in the village. The increase in wealth has been used to bring about a visible improvement in the standard of living. Today most of the houses are screened against flies (a small, but significant innovation), the people are better dressed and many have new kitchens and Hollywood-style bathrooms. Naturally, the number of television sets has increased: in 1960 there were only 12 sets in Farruġ; there are now 73. But even more significant has been the increase in the numbers of Farruġ children who have been able (and encouraged) to gain entry into government secondary schools. In 1960 there were but five boys and two girls attending; today there are 21 boys and 18 girls. The increasing contact between Farruġ and other villages as well as with the conurbation centering on the Grand Harbour is reflected in and a product of the steadily improving public transport system. In 1960 buses made 12 round trips daily between Farruġ and Valletta; by the summer of 1967 these had increased to 27 a day. The cultural gap between town and village is being reduced by these manifest changes, but it has not yet been eliminated.

What of religion and politics, the saints and fireworks with which this book is concerned? Have these too changed? One of the Maltese reviewers of the book thought that one of its main shortcomings was that I had failed to stress that the political and religious factionalism of the rural world about which I wrote, 'although worth recording, is in fact fast becoming a matter of the past' (*Times of Malta*, 3 August 1965). But is this so? It is true that the intensity of the conflict between the Church and the Malta Labour Party has abated considerably. The virulent posters and slogans have disappeared from the walls of church and party club. But the conflict between the two forces again became the key issue during the national elections in 1966 which returned the Church supported Nationalist Party to power with 28 seats to the Malta Labour Party's 22. Though scar-tissue may be forming, the wounds have not yet healed. The villages, as the nation, are still divided politically.

The active clubs in the villages in 1967, as in 1960, were still the band clubs, the Labour clubs and the church associations. Although the Nationalist party established political clubs in many of the villages, most were active only during the election periods. An exception is Kortin, where there is a thriving Nationalist party club. Its success is explained by the political fortunes of Dr Farrugia, old Manwel's son (pp. 52, 112), who has become one of the government's most important ministers.

In Farruġ the Nationalist club opened shortly before the elections and closed soon after. The Labour Party is now centred openly on the Farruġ Stars Football club. This has become the most active club in the village and has moved into the large house on the main square vacated by the baker's family after his death. There is still much bitterness among Labour supporters in the village over the way in which they were opposed by the Church, and in particular by Dun Franġisk, who has since moved on to a large urban parish. Although several attempts have been made by drama enthusiasts to reactivate the amateur theatrical group that had been centred on the Catholic Action hall, Labour supporters still refuse to have anything to do with the hall, which contains the only stage in the village. (In some other villages, such as Marsaxlokk, where parish priests were somewhat more tolerant of differing political opinions, politically mixed theatrical groups are once again using church owned stages.) The Farruġ Catholic Action centre, once so active, has never come to life again. The villagers have not forgotten that Dun Franġisk obliged the children of Labour supporters to sign an oath of loyalty to the Archbishop or leave (pp. 98, 118). Moreover, Labour members of the St Martin club still boycott the festa of their patron, although in 1967 some contributed large sums privately to organizers raising funds for the fireworks.

What of the political saints? In spite of (or more probably because of) its six years in government, the Nationalist Party still draws its strength largely from the patronage based networks of political clients of its prominent members, rather than from its party apparatus. This last, however, has been strengthened by the years of peace and relative prosperity that the Nationalist party and its leader, Dr Giorgio Borg Olivier, have provided. The efficiency with which the Nationalist politicians were able to manipulate their networks of clients, and these latter their political patrons, was one of the important factors responsible for the defeat of all minor political parties in the 1966 election. The short period of independence had demonstrated that these small parties were totally without political influence for those who elected them to office. Thus, in spite of the system of proportional representation, the pragmatic and increasingly sophisticated electorate of independent Malta voted itself a two party system (cf. p. 133).

Many of the inhabitants of Farruġ who demonstrated their loyalty to the Nationalist Party by canvassing votes were rewarded, it is alleged by village Labour supporters, with government jobs. I think it is indeed more than a coincidence that the majority of those who obtained government employment since 1961 were open Nationalist supporters. This suggests that the operation of the political system has changed very little: political saints were if anything more important in 1967 than in 1961. The increasing number of stories and charges of corruption point in the same direction.

Has the rivalry between religious saints and their local opponents become something of the past as my reviewer maintained? In Farruġ it certainly has not. Nor, to judge from the increase in the scale of village festas throughout Malta (and the establishment of two new band clubs in Gozo, Għajnsielem and Nadur), has it in other villages. In point of fact, the festas held during the summer of 1967 were the most elaborate, colourful and crowded that I had ever seen.[1] Friends assured me that my impression was correct: feasts were being celebrated more enthusiastically than ever before. This is chiefly because more money is coming into circulation: now even the village girls, always among the most fervent festa supporters, contribute heavily from their own pay-packets to celebrate their favourite saints. Improving transportation enables relatives, friends and local and even foreign festa enthusiasts to pour into the celebrating village, and to leave it when ever they choose. Festa organizers, aware of their growing public, are working even harder to out do their rivals. Finally, political tension has abated. By the summer of 1967 the bitterness aroused during the 1966 national election had passed. Most villagers enjoyed being able to spend time, energy and money on a well known traditional activity relatively unrelated to national politics. According to informants, celebrating the festa is a way of forgetting past conflict at one level through cooperating with former rivals in a competition at a different level. These are some of the general reasons that helped to make the 1967 festas particularly spectacular.

In Farruġ, the 1967 festa of St Martin, though still boycotted by many Labour members of the band club, was a tremendous success. In fact it compared very favourably with the centenary celebration: many new decorations were bought for the church, the popular demonstration before the feast was as large as in 1960, and the excited participants were carrying many more red scarves, cardboard lions and huge paper umbrellas. Moreover the demonstrators danced in the square for the first time since 1960. Much of the enthusiasm was generated by the excellence

[1] Judging from the unusually large annual crop of complaints to the editor of the English language *Times of Malta*, they were also noisier. These letters were written for the most part by outraged elderly foreign settlers, owners of neurotic dogs, and 'progressive' Maltese who scorn fireworks as the playthings of rustics and the lower orders. I, perhaps foolishly, tried to plead the case for fireworks on behalf of the masses whose English is not up to doing so in public (*Times of Malta*, 22 August 1967). In a virulent counter barrage, intended more to wound than to convince, I was called an 'inane', 'Hitlerian' and 'mindless' defender of an 'outworn custom' for my pains (*Times of Malta*, 29 August 1967)! The polemic salvo proved one of the points that I have stressed in this book, namely that though Malta is small, there are nonetheless considerable differences in the values and customs between the middle-class residents of the towns and the inhabitants of the villages.

of the fireworks. In 1966 the St Martin Club had finally acquired its own (legal) fireworks factory: 1967 was the first year that it came into full production. The fireworkers worked intensively to show their rivals – St Roque supporters as well as neighbouring villages – of what they were capable now that they had proper equipment and storage facilities. Unquestionably the colossal coloured rockets (some weighed just over 14 lbs each!) of the 1967 festa were superior to those of the centenary. During the 1967 festa, too, a considerable number of foreign tourists, attracted by announcements which the organizers had placed in the English language press, found their way to the festa, where they were among the most vocal admirers of the fireworks.

In short, festas, at least in 1967, were very much present and their scale appeared to be growing.

Have the parochial squabbles over decorations, precedence and processions become matters of the past? Not entirely. It is true that the Bishops, reflecting the teachings of the Second Vatican Council (among others that devotions should become more Christ-centred and less saint-centred) have taken some steps to reduce the scale of religious feasts and processions. Yet the effects of their action are not yet noticeable. In fact their attempts to act on these principles in specific situations have intensified existing rivalry. The case of the 1968 Good Friday procession in Rabat, Gozo, is a case in point.

By the end of the summer of 1967 the tensions in the diocese of Gozo described above (pp. 68–69) had abated somewhat. The Apostolic Visitor brought from Rome by the new Bishop (officially still the Apostolic Administrator) of Gozo in an effort to heal the parochial differences, had recommended that the title of Basilica be bestowed upon the collegiate churches of Nadur and Xagħra. The Bishop was again *persona grata* there, and peace seemed restored to the diocese. This unusual tranquillity was shattered in February 1968 when the new Bishop, responding to the recommendations of the Second Vatican Council and his image as a progressive prelate, announced that the traditional Good Friday processions would be transferred to the last two Sundays in Lent because they interfered with the attendance at the services held in churches on Good Friday afternoon. This new regulation played right into the hands of the partisans of Sta Maria in Rabat. For many years these had resented the control

that their rivals, the supporters of St George, had been able to
exercise over the Good Friday procession because most of the
statues for the procession were housed in the church of St George.
By forbidding the procession to be held on Good Friday, the
Bishop abolished the exclusive position the St George supporters
derived from their control over it. Sta Maria supporters were
quick to take advantage of the opportunity the Bishop's new
regulations offered them: they petitioned for and received permission to organize a Good Friday type procession from their
church, the cathedral, on one of the last two Sundays in Lent.
There would be two processions before Easter henceforth.

The leaders of the St George partit reacted in a way that any
attentive reader of this book could have predicted: they cancelled
their traditional Good Friday procession (which had been transferred to Palm Sunday), and announced that they were also
cancelling the external celebration of the annual festa of St
George in July. Instead of the festa they held an elaborate song
festival with invited pop stars from more than a dozen countries.
Moreover, to ensure as little interest as possible in the new procession of Sta Maria on Passion Sunday (and, to be sure, to annoy
the Bishop), they hired a beat group to give a public programme
while the procession was taking place.

I leave it to the reader to decide whether parochial clashes
such as those I described in the book have become matters of the
past.

The changes, being instituted as a result of the Second Vatican
Council will, probably in time, bring about changes in the way
in which religion in Malta is articulated with the social structure.
But the time I spent in Malta during the summer of 1967 was too
brief to attempt to assess these. It is certain that many who have
been among the faithful supporters of the policy of the Bishops
are now beginning to ask questions in private and in public: The
regulation of the size of families, the place of fireworks and processions, the degree to which the church should enforce its political views, the expenditure of funds on church decorations, the
voice that laymen and women should have in parish and diocese,
the uses to which the Church's great wealth should be put, are
some of the many topics being discussed.

Aggiornamento, modernization, is taking place in Malta everywhere, not only in the religious sphere. Some of its directions

12

have been touched upon above, but a more profound discussion will have to follow more intensive research than I have been able to carry out to date. Though changing, the principles of social action described for the early sixties still remain very much in evidence in rural Malta eight years later.

Appendix A

Festa and Band Club Partiti

	Titular Feast	Band Club	Secondary Feast	Band Club
A. FESTA AND BAND CLUB RIVALRY				
GHAXAQ	The Assumption	'St. Mary'	St. Joseph	'St. Joseph'
GUDJA[1]	O/L of the Rosary	'La Stella'	O/L of Consolation	'O/L of Consolation'
KIRKOP	St. Leonard	'St. Leonard'	St. Joseph	'St. Joseph'
LUQA	St. Andrew	'St. Andrew'	O/L of Consolation	'Union'
MQABBA	The Assumption	'King George V'	O/L of the Lily	'Lily'
QRENDI	The Assumption	'St. Mary'	O/L of Lourdes	'Lourdes'
RABAT	St. Paul	'Count Roger'	St. Joseph[2] (Franciscans)	'L'Isle Adam'
VITTORIOSA	St. Lawrence	'Duke of Edinburgh'	St. Dominic[2] (Dominicans)	'Prince of Wales'
ŻEBBUĠ	St. Philip	'St. Philip' 'St. Philip's Festivities and Social Club'	St. Joseph	'De Rohan'
ŻURRIEQ	St. Catherine	'St. Catherine'	O/L of Mount Carmel	'Queen Victoria'
B. INTER PARISH AND BAND CLUB RIVALRY				
QORMI	St. George	'St. George'	St. Sebastian	'Pinto'
RABAT, GOZO	The Assumption	'Leone'	St. George	'La Stella'
SLIEMA	Stella Maris	'Stella Maris'	Sacred Heart	'Sliema'
VALLETTA	St. Paul	'La Vallette'	St. Dominic[3] (Dominicans)	'King's Own'

[1] Both saints are secondary; the titular is the Assumption of Our Lady.

[2] The devotion is centred on a church in the parish that is run by regular clergy. The rivalry is thus classified midway between A and B.

[3] Though this is the main feast, the titular of the parish is Our Lady of Porto Salvo.

C. BAND CLUB RIVALRY ONLY

BIRKIRKARA	St. Helen	'St. Helen'	X	'Duke of Connaught'
HAMRUN	St. Gajetan	'St. Gajetan'	X	'St. Joseph'
MELLIEHA	Nativity of Our Lady	'La Vittoria'	X	'Imperial'
ŻABBAR[1]	O/L of Grace	'Maria M. Gratiae'	(St. Michael)	'St. Michael'
ŻEJTUN	St. Catherine	'Beland'	X	'Żejtun'

D. FESTA RIVALRY EXISTED FORMERLY

BALZAN	The Annunciation	'St. Gabriel'	St. Valentine	X
DINGLI	The Assumption	X	National Feast on September 8	'Dingli Club'[2]
GHARGHUR	St. Bartholomew	'St. Bartholomew'[2]	St. Joseph	X
LIJA	Transfiguration of Our Lord	'Pius X'	St. Aloysius	X
NAXXAR	Nativity of Our Lady	'Peace'	O/L of Doctrine	X
SAFI	The Conversion of St. Paul	'St. Paul'[2]	O/L of the Rosary	X
SIĠĠIEWI	St. Nicholas	'St. Nicholas'	St. Joseph	X

[1] The external feast of the secondary saint was suppressed.
[2] Social and festa club without a band.

Appendix B

Extracts from the 1962 Electoral Manifesto of the Malta Labour Party[1]

The Malta Labour Party reaffirm their democratic socialist principles which do not run counter to Christian beliefs and solemnly subscribe to:

(1) the right of every nation, however small, to govern itself and to determine its own international relations in its own best interest and for the furtherance of its own progress and prosperity.

(2) freedom of conscience. This ensures for every citizen the right to exercise his own religious beliefs without hindrance and at the same time to fulfil his civic duties without pseudo-religious interference.

(3) the equality of all citizens before the law of the land. This implies not only the adherence to the Charter of Human Rights but also the abolition of medieval privileges which have retarded our own social and economic progress. Any interference with the right of a democratically elected majority to implement the people's mandate is a crime.

(4) equal opportunities to all citizens. This entails freedom of speech at public meetings, in the press, on the air, universal suffrage, free compulsory education, full employment and adequate social services from the cradle to the grave. Whilst the right to private ownership is by no means denied, the state must exercise the positive function of preventing any individual or group of individuals from dominating the heights of the nation's economy and dictating living standards to their fellow citizens. The Malta Labour Party firmly believe in the right of the people to have the final say in the nation's vital means of production. All forms

[1] Source: *The Voice of Malta*, 7 and 14 January 1962.

of Co-operative and Social ownership should therefore be encouraged in order to curb the excesses of unbridled capitalism.

(5) Charter of the United Nations and the equality of all the human races – black, white or coloured. In particular Maltese Labour believe in the right of every nation to choose the method of government and the social system most consonant with its economic environment and its special political and social stage of development. The division of the world into two huge power blocs, the one intent on destroying the other, militates against world peace and the brotherhood of man. Whilst therefore communism with its anti-democratic suppression of freedom of conscience, freedom of association and other restrictive human rights earns Labour's unequivocal condemnation, the means chosen so far to combat it – namely nuclear weapons and military alliances are equally reprehensible. Labour believe in a reinvigorated United Nation's Organization able to enforce the principles embodied in the Charter through an international police force.

II. INDEPENDENCE

Since time immemorial our islands have been dominated by foreign powers. Our people have not therefore been the custodians of these fundamental human rights. On the contrary our social, political and economic institutions have been at the mercy of foreign masters who have fashioned them to suit their own requirements. . . .

Bibliography

I. SOURCES RELATING TO MALTA

The best bibliographical sources for Malta are Beeley (1959), Price (1954) and Smith (1953). The following Bibliography contains only works consulted in the preparation of this book.

ABELA, F. G., and CIANTAR, G., 1772, 1780. *Malta Illustrata*, 2 vols. Malta.
'Acts of the Apostles', *New Testament*.
ARMSTRONG, A. H., 1945. 'Malta and the Siege of 1940–1942', *Downside Review*, LXIII, 158–70.
AQUILINA, JOSEPH, 1959. *The Structure of Maltese*. Valletta.
— — 1961. *Papers in Maltese Linguistics*. Valletta.
ARCHIEPISCOPAL CURIA, 1933, 1934. *Annuario della Diocesi di Malta*, 1933. Malta.
A.S.V.S., 1930. 'Malta: Church and State', *Foreign Affairs*, IX, 157–60.
BADGER, G. PERCY, 1872. *Historical Guide to Malta and Gozo*. 5th ed., Malta.
BARTOLO, SIR AUGUSTUS, 1930. 'The Present Position of Malta', *Journal of the Royal Institute of International Affairs*, IX (Sept.).
BEELEY, BRIAN W., 1959. *A Bibliography of the Maltese Islands: Provisional Draft*. Mimeographed. University of Durham.
— — 1960. 'The Farmer in Changing Rural Society in Malta'. Unpublished Ph.D. dissertation. University of Durham.
BOISGELIN DE KERDU, PIERRE MARIE LOUIS DE, 1804. *Ancient and Modern Malta*. 2 vols. London.
BOWEN-JONES, H., DEWDNEY, J. C., and FISHER, W. B., 1961. *Malta: Background for Development*. University of Durham.
BRADLEY, R. N., 1912. *Malta and the Mediterranean Race*. London.
BRYDONE, P., 1840. *A Tour Through Sicily and Malta*. Edinburgh.
BUSUTTIL, E. D., 1949. *Kalepin (Dizjunarju): Malti – Ingliż*. 2nd ed.; Valletta.
— — 1952. *Kalepin (Dizjunarju): Ingliż – Malti*. Malta.
BUSUTTIL, V., 1894. *Holiday Customs in Malta*. Malta.
BUTCHER, MAY, 1938. *Elements of Maltese*. Oxford.
BUTTIĠIEĠ, ANTON, 1954. *Is-Santwarju Nazzjonali tal-Madonna Tal-Kunċizzioni. Qala*. Malta.
BUXTON, L. H. D., 1922. 'The Ethnology of Malta', *Journal of the Royal Anthropological Society*, LII, 164–211.

BUXTON, L. H. D., 1924. 'Malta: An Anthropographical Study', *Geographical Review*, XIV (Jan.), 75–87.

CALLUS, Rev. PHILIP, 1961. *The Rising of the Priests*. Malta.

CARUANA, V., and MIZZI, FORTUNATO, 1948. 'Agricultural Law in Malta', *The Law Journal*, II (Oct.) 115–37.

CASSAR PULLICINO, JOSEPH, 1951. 'Maltese Customs and Beliefs in 1575', *Folk-Lore*, LXII (Sept.), 398–404.

—— 1956. 'La Settimana Santa a Malta', *Phoenix*, II (Jan.–June), 1–24.

—— 1956. 'Social Aspects of Maltese Nicknames', *Scientia*, XXII, 66–94.

—— 1956. 'Malta in 1575: Social Aspects of an Apostolic Visit', *Melita Historica*, II, 19–41.

CASTAGNA, P. P., 1880, 1890. *Lis-Storia Ta Malta*. 3 vols. Valletta.

CENTRE DE RECHERCHES SOCIO-RELIGIEUSES. 1960. *The Socio-Religious Study of Malta and Gozo*. Mimeographed. Bruxelles.

CHARLTON, W. A., 1960. 'Recent Trends in the Economic Geography of Malta'. Unpublished Ph.D. dissertation. University of Durham.

CONCILIUM REGIONALE MELITENSE, 1935. *Decreta*. Malta.

Critien's Malta Almanac, 1870–1910. Malta.

ETON, WILLIAM, 1803. *Authentic Materials for a History of the Principality of Malta*. London.

FERRES, ACHILLE, 1866. *Descrizione Storica delle Chiese di Malta e Gozo*. Malta.

GALEA, JOSEPH, 1937. *Il-Qima ta' San Vittorju Martri Fin-Naxxar*. Malta.

—— 1944. *Il-Parroċċa ta' San Pawl Naufragu Tal-Belt Valletta*. Malta.

—— 1946. *Storja ta' Santa Marija ta' Birmiftuħ. Il-Gudja*. Malta.

—— 'Storja Dokumentata tas-Sodalita tal-Erwieħ'. Unpublished manuscript lent by the author.

General Guide to Malta and Gozo, 1912–1940. Valletta: Muscat and Malta Herald.

GENTILHOMME FRANÇAIS, 1679. *Nouvelle Relation du Voyage et Description exacte de L'Isle de Malthe*. Paris.

SOCIAL ACTION MOVEMENT, 1961. *Ghawdex Jiddefendi L-Knisja*, Gozo.

GUIGNARD, FRANÇOIS EMMANUEL DE, Comte de Saint–Priest, 1791. *Malte Par un Voyageur François*. n.p.

HANCOCK, W. K., 1937. *Survey of British Commonwealth Affairs*. Vol. I. Oxford.

HARDIMAN, WILLIAM, 1909. *A History of Malta*. London.

HARDING, MR. JUSTICE WILLIAM, 1942. *The Revised Edition of the Laws of Malta*. 6 vols. Malta.

KININMONTH, CHRISTOPHER, 1957. *The Brass Dolphins*. London.

LAFERLA, A. V., 1945, 1947. *British Malta*. 2 vols. Malta.

—— 1958. *The Story of Man in Malta*. 3rd ed. Malta.

LUKE, SIR HARRY, 1949. *Malta: An Appreciation*. London.

MALTA GOVERNMENT, 1821. *Proclamations, Minutes and Other Official Notes.* I (5 Oct. 1813–31 Dec. 1820). Malta.

—— 1843. *Ordinances and other Official Acts*, VIII (1 Jan. 1836–Dec. 1841). Malta.

—— *Census Reports for the years 1843, 1851, 1861–1931, 1948* and *1957.*

—— 1961. *Statistical Abstract of the Maltese Islands, 1960* Valletta.

—— *Government Gazette.* Valletta.

MALTA LABOUR PARTY. '1962 Electoral Manifesto of the Malta Labour Party', *The Voice of Malta* (Jan. 7 and 14 1962).

M.C.D., 1876. *A Short Sketch of the Maltese Nobility.* Valletta.

MEJLAK, MARY, 1958. *Nokkla Sewda.* Malta.

MIÈGE, M. 1840. *Histoire de Malte.* 3 vols. Paris.

MIFSUD BONNICI, ROBERT, 1951. *Mużiċisti Kompożituri.* Malta.

—— 1954. *Ġrajja Tal-Mużika F'Malta U Ghawdex.* Malta.

—— 1956, 1957. *Ġrajja Ta' Baned F'Malta U Ghawdex.* 2 vols. Malta.

MINTOFF, DOM, 1960. *Il-Principji Fundamentali tal-Partit tal-Haddiema.* Malta.

—— 1961. *Priests and Politics.* Malta.

MITCHELL, PETER K., 1959. *Studies in the Agrarian Geography of Malta.* 2 vols. Mimeographed. University of Durham.

MOLSON, HUGH, 1934. 'The Problems of Malta', *Quarterly Review*, CCLXIII (July), 127–43.

MONTANARO, EDGAR G., 1942. *Storia della Venda. Arciconfraterntià del Ssmo. Rosario e della Misericordia.* Malta.

Muirs Malta Almanac, 1857, 1858. Malta.

NAXXAR, 1930. 'The Situation in Malta', *English Review.* LI (Oct.), 475–83.

NEWMAN, E. W. POLSON, 1940. 'Church and State in Malta', *Empire Review*, LII (Aug.), 108–15.

PAGE, GEO. ALFRED, 1892. *A Guide to the Laws and Regulations of Malta.* Malta.

PARLIAMENTARY PAPERS AND REPORTS

—— 1880. *Report on the Educational System of Malta by P. J. Keenan.* C-2685, Vol. XLIX. London.

—— 1912. *Report of the Royal Commission on the Finances, Economic Position, and Judicial Procedure of Malta.* Cmnd. 6090. London.

—— 1930. *Correspondence with the Holy See relative to Maltese Affairs, January 1929–May 1930.* Blue Book. Cmnd. 3588. London.

—— 1932. *Report of the Malta Royal Commission, 1931.* Cmnd. 3993. London.

—— 1961. *Report of the Malta Constitutional Commission, 1960.* Cmnd. 1261. London.

PRICE, CHARLES A., 1954. *Malta and the Maltese. A Study in Nineteenth Century Migration.* Melbourne.

RANSIJAT, JEAN DE BOSREDON, 1801. *Journal du Siège et Blocus De Malte.* An IX. Paris.

RESEARCH AGENCY MALTA, 1960. *The Parish of Floriana. Report on a Mail Questionnaire.* Mimeographed. Valletta.

RICHARDSON, MICHAEL, 1960. 'Aspects of the Demography of Modern Malta'. Unpublished Ph.D. dissertation. University of Durham.

RYAN, FREDRICK W., 1910. *Malta*. London.

SANDYS, GEORGE, 1615. *A Relation of a Journey Begun AD 1610*. London.

SCICLUNA, HANNIBAL, 1923. *Documents Relating to the French Occupation of Malta*. Malta.

SEDDAL, REV. HENRY, 1870. *Malta, Past and Present*. London.

SHAW, CLAUDIUS, 1875. *Malta 'Sixty Years Ago'*. London.

SHEPARD, ERIC, 1926. *Malta and Me*. London.

SMITH, HARRISON, 1953. *Britain in Malta*. 2 vols. Malta.

TORTELL, PHILIP, 1961. 'Sliema: A Modern Town'. Unpublished undergraduate dissertation, St. Michael's College. Malta.

VATICAN, HOLY SEE, 1930. *Exposition of the Malta Question with Documents, February 1929–June 1930*. White Book. Vatican City.

VELLA, CHARLES G., ed., 1958. *The Catholic Directory of Malta and Gozo*. Valletta.

VELLA, E. B., 1927. *Storja Taż-Żejtun u Marsaxlokk*. Malta.

—— 1930. *Storja tal-Mosta bil-Knisja Tagħha*. Malta.

—— 1934. *Storja ta' Birkirkara, bil-Kolleġġata Tagħha*. Malta.

—— 1945. *L'Arċikonfraternita ta' San Ġużepp Fir-Rabat tal-Imdina*. Malta.

WILKINSON, CHARLES, 1804. *Epitome of the History of Malta and Gozo*. London.

ZAMMIT, REV. LAURENZ, 1927. *Descrizioni Storica tal Cnisia Parrochiali tal Imkabba*. Hamrun.

II. OTHER WORKS CITED

ADDIS, WILLIAM E., and others, 1960. 'Archbishop', in *A Catholic Dictionary*. 17th ed.; pp. 44 f. London.

ANDERSON, GALLATIN, 1956. 'A Survey of Italian Godparenthood', in *Kroeber Anthropological Society Papers*, No. 15. Berkeley.

CAMARA, FERNANDO, 1952. 'Religious and Political Organization', in *Heritage of Conquest*, pp. 142–73. Sol Tax, ed. Glencoe.

GLUCKMAN, MAX, 1959. *Custom and Conflict in Africa*. Oxford.

KENNY, MICHAEL, 1960. 'Patterns of Patronage in Spain', *Anthropological Quarterly*, XXXIII (Jan.), 14–23.

—— 1961. *A Spanish Tapestry*. London.

MAIR, LUCY, 1962. *Primitive Government*. London.

MINTZ, SIDNEY W., and WOLF, ERIC R., 1950. 'An Analysis of Ritual Coparenthood (Compadrazgo)', *Southwestern Journal of Anthropology*, VI, 341–68.

PITRÈ, GIUSEPPE, 1900. *Feste Patronali in Sicilia*. Vol. XXI of *Biblioteca delle Tradizioni Populari Siciliane*. Torino.

PITT-RIVERS, J. A., 1954. *The People of the Sierra*. London.

Index

14-202